WORDS THAT CIRCLED THE WORLD

CEN/Pon

'THIS REMARKABLE BOOK... IS A RICH BLEND
OF INSIGHT, SANITY, WISDOM AND HUMOUR'
JOHN STOTT

WORDS THAT CIRCLED THE WORLD

A CHRISTIAN'S RESPONSE TO 13 QUOTATIONS THAT SHAPED OUR TIMES

RICHARD BEWES

Christian Focus

ISBN 1-85792-812-1

© Copyright Richard Bewes 2002

Published in 2002
by
Christian Focus Publications, Ltd.
Geanies House, Fearn, Tain,
Ross-shire, IV20 1TW, Great Britain.

Part of this book previously published as
Great Quoations from the Twentieth Century
in 1999 by Christian Focus Publications

www.christianfocus.com

Cover Design by Alister MacInnes

Printed and bound by
MFP, Manchester

Contents

Foreword

What on earth have Rudolph Giuliani, Marilyn Monroe, Mahatma Ghandi, Princess Diana, Billy Graham and other notables of the last hundred years got in common?
Answer: they all uttered memorable epigrams which Richard Bewes has picked up and explored in this remarkable book.

He has a profound knowledge of Scripture, a close understanding of the contemporary world and an uncanny knack of finding points of contact between the two.

Richard Bewes and I have been friends, neighbours and colleagues for many years. So I know that *Words That Circled the World* is an expression of his personal integrity. I warmly recommend it to anybody who wants to probe the basic issues of life. It is well conceived, well researched and well written. Readers will find in it, as I have done, a rich blend of insight, sanity, wisdom and humour, with Jesus Christ himself always at the centre.

JOHN STOTT

Introduction

It was a colleague, Richard Trist of Melbourne, who suggested the idea for this book, and I am grateful for his encouragement. Naturally over the past decades there have been numbers of men and women whose specific utterance, at some point, gained massive publicity and then became familiar to millions of people. In this way, either they, or the events that defined them, took on a kind of timeless status. The *Titanic* was one such event. September 11th, 2001 was another.

I have selected thirteen quotations that would be instantly recognisable by vast numbers of people, and then – without doing an injustice to their source – attempted a Christian comment on them.

We are challenged to be living at a time of breathtaking transition in our twenty-first century. And the exercise of looking back a little should help us prepare for the unknown future. History invariably helps. Our society these days – from top politicians and media controllers downwards – seems to be suffering from a devastating corporate memory loss. But as my saintly mother said to me long ago in a letter, 'You simply cannot be educated unless you know some history'.

I write this book out of gratitude for the two world public figures, man and woman, whom I consider to have been the greatest inspirers of all in these past momentous decades – Billy and Ruth Graham of Montreat, North Carolina.

RICHARD BEWES
Written at All Souls Church,
Langham Place, London

1

'Yes, lady, God himself could not sink this ship'

(Southampton, 10 April 1912)

The Rev. J. Stuart Holden, thirty-eight years of age, faced a problem as he woke at his London vicarage on Tuesday, 9 April 1912. *To sail or not to sail?* A celebrated preacher in his own Anglican church of St Paul's Portman Square, he was in wide demand as a speaker at events such as the famed Keswick Convention in the North of England. His speaking trips had taken him across the Atlantic no less than thirty-five times, and he was about to embark on a thirty-sixth.

He was alone in the house. Unexpectedly his wife had been taken into hospital, and was facing an operation. Once more, Stuart gazed at the ticket that was staring up at him. It read:

Rev. J. Stuart Holden

WHITE STAR LINE

YOUR ATTENTION IS SPECIALLY DRAWN TO THE CONDITIONS OF TRANSPORTATION IN THE ENCLOSED CONTRACT. THE COMPANY'S LIABILITY FOR BAGGAGE IS STRICTLY LIMITED, BUT PASSENGERS CAN PROTECT THEMSELVES BY INSURANCE.

First Class Passenger Ticket per Steamship 'Titanic'

SAILING FROM 10/4/1912

There was no question about it, reflected Stuart. With his wife in hospital he would have to cancel his passage and forgo the maiden voyage of the biggest, most glamorous ship ever built. With a sigh he picked up the telephone.

Days later he was reading his own obituary in the press! Guided by the passengers' list, the newspapers had included

Stuart Holden's name as among those drowned in the greatest of all sea disasters, the sinking of *The Titanic,* only four days out from Southampton. For the rest of his Christian ministry, Stuart Holden kept his unused ticket framed in his study, as a reminder of his debt to Providence. His church of St Paul's Portman Square, later known as St Paul's Robert Adam Street, was to become sister to our own church of All Souls, Langham Place, within a single united parish.

Yes, lady, God himself could not sink this ship...
It is ironic that these words from one of the deck hands should have been spoken to a Christian missionary, Sylvia Caldwell, who, with her husband Albert, was travelling second class, having returned from Thailand where the couple had been teaching at the Bangkok Christian College. With their baby boy Albert – who would be wrapped in a blanket on the fateful night of 15 April – they lived to tell the tale, and so provide the world with one of the memorable quotes of the twentieth century.

The stunning tragedy of *The Titanic* signalled an end to the age of unbroken optimism in the Western world, and put up a marker. It posed the question, 'What things can we be sure of in this fragile cockleshell of our existence?' It pressed the issue, 'What things really *matter,* when the stairs under your feet on the grand staircase don't feel quite right, when the deck is beginning to slope at an angle – but not yet to the extent that you could draw attention to it without seeming a little, well, *tactless?'*

The Titanic imprinted itself upon the collective memory of our whole family – if for no other reason than that my mother at the age of nine, together with her four sisters and her brother, stood at Sea View on the Isle of Wight, watching and waving as the giant liner, eleven stories high and a sixth of a mile long, came gliding past them, never to be seen again. They never forgot that first and last sight.

I know all the stories and the quotes backwards.

From the bridge – *'What do you see?'* – *'Iceberg right ahead!'* The calm acknowledgement – *'Thank you!'* The flimsy reassurances – *'There's talk of an iceberg, Ma'am.'* The banalities – *'There is your beautiful nightdress gone.'*

The lifeboats and deck-chairs; the fate of Lady Astor's jewels (and fifteen hundred missing persons); the band on deck playing ragtime, and then *Nearer My God to Thee* as the great ship began its two-mile slide down – *The Titanic* was to become a universal symbol of the twentieth century's loss of confidence in safe, copper-bottomed values and institutions, and in our human capacity to govern our destinies.

When the crystal chandeliers are hanging at a tilt, when they're winching down the lifeboats – but only enough for half the passengers – what *matters* at that moment more than anything else in the world? What counts as a valuable to be salvaged? Plenty of incidents in the early hours of 15 April illustrated the age-old principle expressed in the challenge of Christ: **What good is it for a man to gain the whole world, yet forfeit his soul? Or what can a man give in exchange for his soul?** (Mark 8:36–37).

A crisis, whether on *The Titanic* or not, is enough to highlight the issue, and turn our distorted human values on their heads. A chemist from Toronto, Major Arthur Peuchen, paused in his first-class cabin as he wondered what to take with him from the stricken liner. Eventually he left behind a tin box containing $200,000 in bonds and $100,000 in preferred stock – and stepped out onto the freezing deck clutching just three oranges.

There's second class passenger Stuart Collett, a young theological student, leaving everything behind except the Bible he had promised his brother he would always carry until they met again. Like Peuchen, he survived.

Everything is topsy-turvy in a crisis. Your sense of time gets skewed, for one thing. It becomes stretched – from the moment of the unwelcome phone call at 6.00am onwards. Later in the day you think it's 4.00pm and are amazed to discover that it's only 11 o'clock in the morning. Reactions vary too, as they did on *The Titanic*. 'At 12.15 it was hard to know whether to joke or be serious – whether to chop down a door and be a hero, or chop it down and get arrested.'[1]

'Man, are you saved?' asked the Glasgow preacher, John Harper, of a fellow Scot as they both struggled in the sub-zero water, holding onto pieces of wreck.

'No, I am not,' came the reply.

'Believe on the Lord Jesus Christ and you will be saved!' urged Harper.

The waves took the preacher away, but a little later he was washed back alongside his companion.

'Are you saved now?' he persisted.

'No, I cannot honestly say that I am.'

Once more Harper repeated the Scripture sentence, 'Believe on the Lord Jesus Christ, and you will be saved'. Then, losing his hold, he sank.

As the young Scot later told a meeting in Hamilton, Canada, 'And there, alone in the night,

---

1. Walter Lord, *A Night to Remember*, Corgi Books.

and with two miles of water under me, I believed. *I am John Harper's last convert.'*

The 'John Harper Memorial Church' can be visited in Glasgow today; there is also a memorial at the Moody Church in Chicago, in commemoration of an outstanding ambassador of the Christian Gospel.

What good is it for a man to gain the whole world, yet forfeit his soul? Or what can a man give in exchange for his soul? As Jesus spoke these words to the crowd around him, he was drawing a contrast between two things. Not, as we might suppose, between the present and the future. He was not asking what good it would be for someone to gain the present and lose the future. Certainly, the person who gains the fleeting present and loses the eternal future has made a bad bargain, but that is not the contrast implied here. Actually the New Testament never teaches that if we lose our soul we shall even gain the fleeting present. Certainly we would lose the future, but Christ never suggested for a moment that we would gain even the present by making it the focus of our ambitions.

At the same time, the people who save their life for all eternity don't lose the *present!* On the basis of Jesus' teaching, the eternal future is gained, but they also gain the best in this *present* life too. Such is the teaching of the Scriptures.

But just supposing that I, as a Christian, was wrong, and that my materialist critic was right? That there was no spiritual dimension, no God, no Christ, no soul that needed saving, no settling up at the end. *Just supposing?*

In such a case I must still maintain that I end up with the advantage. I put this once to a London cab driver as he took me to a wedding.

'I feel so sorry for people like you,' he had announced over his shoulder. 'There you are with your Bibles and your churches, and looking forward to some comfort and reward at the end of all your effort – only to get there and find that there was nothing there at all!' He began to shake with laughter.

I laughed too. But then I turned the tables on my unbelieving chauffeur.

'But just supposing you are right and that I'm deluded,' I countered. 'Even then I end up ahead of you! Here I am, convinced – in my delusion – that life isn't the product of chance; believing – in my delusion – that I'm here for a purpose and that a man called Jesus has overcome evil and death and has forgiven me my sins and given me eternal life and an underlying confidence! *And then,* if you as a materialist are right, I finally die and go out like a light – and don't even have the disappointment of knowing that I was deluded!

'But what about *you?*' I continued. 'If I'm right and *you* are wrong, without question you're the loser! There you are, living off your own batteries, trying to make sense of this short life, staving off ill health as best you can and keeping as cheerful as possible, until your energies fade and you die. And then you are in for the most appalling shock – when you will be confronted by the very person you've ignored all your life, and are made to realise that everything you lived for ended in waste and total loss. Just supposing such things can be enough to turn someone's thinking around.' We parted friends, as I got off the taxi for the wedding.

We don't have to stay in a *just suppose* mindset, however. There is enough solid data in the life, deeds, teaching and claims of Jesus Christ to have created the biggest family of faith that the world has ever seen. It is to be found on every continent; in every country, from Iceland to Antarctica, from Fiji in the Pacific to the Greenwich Meridian Line in London. It is, actually, the only truly *world* faith that there has ever been. Every day some 100,000 new believers are added. Every week some sixteen or seventeen hundred new congregations come into being, that were not in existence previously. All told, there are around two billion people who, in one way or another, come at least nominally under the banner of Jesus Christ. In addition there must be many more secret believers and underground fellowships in countries where Christian belief and practice are firmly banned.

It takes the prospect of martyrdom, or a crisis like *The Titanic,* to bring the issue of life and eternity – and of our human response to Christ's claims – into clear focus. But, emphatically, it is not the future and the present that are in contrast. According to the teaching of Christ in Mark 8:36–37, the contrast is between *the World* and *the Soul.*

The world! The tangible, material world and all it contains: wealth, success, power, gadgets, pleasure, educational advancement, business promotion, reputation – everything, in fact, that appeals to the senses; the things we eat, see, do, possess and experience.

There is nothing intrinsically wrong in those things by themselves, unless – by riveting our main attention upon *them,* we lose sight of what Jesus says outweighs everything else, namely, *the soul.* The soul! The real, irreplaceable *You* that thinks, plans, decides, wills, weeps, dreams and worships. Which is the more important – the world or the soul? It's quite clear that the greatest Teacher of all time regards the *soul* – our basic person and character – the true and unique personality that each of us comprise – as of far more worth than any accumulation of material gain or fleeting sensual experiences.

Wealth meant so little on that freezing April night in the Atlantic. Much might have been made, at other times, of wealthy John Jacob Astor, and Mrs Astor's lost jewellery; or of Mrs Widener's pearls; or of the Ryerson family on board *The Titanic,* with their sixteen trunks all floating in the ship's hold; of the valets, nurses, governesses and paid companions – all there to make life easier for someone. But not on that night! There is nothing like the prospect of a ship going down within the hour to concentrate the mind on what is really important.

True, you could still have had quite a good time, and even a little fun, in that short hour, if you chose to ignore the impending disaster. You could break off a piece of iceberg for your highball, or turn up the ragtime, louder... faster...

'Everyone who is in Third Class, you can now go into the First Class section!'

'Drinks? Yeah, they're free from now on!'

'You want to play football in the First Class dining room? Go right ahead; it's okay about the chandeliers!'

But in an hour the ship will be at the bottom of the ocean.

There's something about treating the world as a pleasure cruise that is basically unsatisfying to the human spirit. To side with the *consumers* of society, rather than with the *contributors;* to have joined the good-timers, and to end one's days with a collection of memories only; nothing done of any lasting worth – and with a moral character about the size of a peapod – *we were not born for that.*

It was with wistfulness that Charles Darwin, the great scientist of the nineteenth century, wrote to an acquaintance, J.D. Hooker, on 17 June 1868. It appears that in earlier life Darwin had had some connection with the Christian faith, but these ties had become ever looser with the passing years. The letter included this admission:

> I am glad you were at *The Messiah.* It is the one thing I should like to hear again. But I dare say I should find my soul too dried up to appreciate it as in olden days. For it is a horrid bore, to feel as I constantly do, that I am a withered leaf, for everything, except science.

Dried up...a horrid bore. Surely we are more valuable than that! The soul...the unique being that every person is – why are we valuable in ourselves?

The Christian answer is twofold. We are valuable first by right of Creation and secondly by right of Redemption. We were *made* in the image of God, then – subsequent to our rebellion against the Creator – we were *bought* by the love of God through the Cross of Jesus Christ. *Who are we?* There are life-changing answers to that question!

The Titanic was a terrible disaster that left its stamp upon the whole of the momentous twentieth century. If it made any kind of a positive impact upon our race, it did, perhaps, help great numbers of men and women to *think:*

If the best piece of technology we had ever come up with is so fragile, what are we all about? What are we here for? What is the matter with us? Where are the things that can last? How can I as an individual survive and live on?

Let's not wait for our own personal crisis to hit before finding answers! Those who survived the ordeal of 15 April 1912 never forgot it – the muffled thuds, the crashing of those five grand pianos, the tinkle of breaking glass and then the final roar as everything broke loose; the crockery, the fittings, 30,000 eggs, the crystal chandeliers and myriads of abandoned valuables.

Don't wait for your own crisis. It is the Cross, supremely, that faces us with the definitive crisis and decision of our lives, that challenges us to respond to the Christ who died to win us forgiveness and eternal life. The stark events of our rocking, reeling world come as a reminder of his sobering message: **A man's life, a woman's life, does not consist in the abundance of things that they possess.**

The only thing we are going to take out at the end of our lives is our character. What will have happened to it by then? It is stories of people like Sylvia Caldwell, Stuart Holden and John Harper which can help us to find the answer.

2

'I have in my hand a piece of paper'

(British Prime Minister, Neville Chamberlain, 1938)

'At 2.30 we were again attacked by two submarines; both of them are supposed to be chasing us now. I actually saw the torpedo miss us by inches (the captain said about 10 feet only) – a great red thing splashing through the water. As we watched it, fascinated and horrified, we saw that it had indeed missed us but was aiming straight at a big grey boat behind us in the convoy. Our boat, The Malda, hooted violently, and to our joy and amazement we saw the big grey boat swerve to the side, and the torpedo just miss its bows. Shortly afterwards we just missed a torpedo on our other side.

A few moments later, a violent explosion told us that one of the boats in our convoy was torpedoed – a big oil tanker to our right – with her side ripped right out. She listed right over in the water, and the last we saw of her was a thick cloud of smoke. A destroyer went to her aid and the crew got into their boats safely. We have altered course and are going out west to the Atlantic in the hopes of eluding the submarines.

We are in another, safer, cabin tonight, near the top deck, and everyone is sleeping in their clothes with life-belts at hand. I have packed the rucksack with the kids' shoes and overcoats, and all are wearing identification discs. The men passengers, under Cecil, have organised a special "look-out" watch for submarines all night and all day.

"Kept by the power of God" – that's been my special thought all day – and now I'm going to sleep. Heaps of love darlings; God keep you going too.

Your loving Sylvia'

My mother's letter – written from the Atlantic during World War II – still makes my spine tingle as I read it. I was one of the 'kids', aged four, and 'Cecil' was my missionary father, booked onto the British India Line ship *The Malda,* for another term of missionary service in my country of birth, Kenya, as war broke out. The hazardous journey in the zigzagging convoy of forty ships left an impression on our family that has stayed with us for life. Hitler was the trouble centre for everything. Only when the voyage was over did we children find the courage to run around, wearing little 'Hitler' masks that we had devised. The associations of that sinister name have remained with me always.

With hindsight it is all too easy to look back and wonder with amazement how civilised governments at that time could contemplate any kind of a deal with a man who came to be recognised by millions as the pariah of the twentieth century. It was British Prime Minister, Neville Chamberlain, who, at the time of the 1938 Munich meeting with Hitler and the Italian leader Mussolini, accepted Hitler's word at its face value and achieved a peace accord. It was obtained by part of Czechoslovakia being handed over to the ever-grasping Adolf Hitler. The quote attributed to Chamberlain at that time is, *I trust Adolf Hitler.*

Chamberlain arrived back in London, holding what eventually transpired to be a worthless piece of paper. His return from Munich was hailed with rapture and relief by the crowd that greeted him off the plane. *'I have in my hand a piece of paper!'* cried Chamberlain as he held up the agreement before the press cameras:

> We, the German Führer and Chancellor and the British Prime Minister, have had a further meeting today and are agreed in recognising that the question

of Anglo-German relations is of the first importance for the two countries and for Europe.

We regard the agreement signed last night and the Anglo-German Naval Agreement as symbolic of the desire of our two peoples never to go to war with one another again.

We are resolved that the method of consultation shall be the method adopted to deal with any other questions that may concern our two countries; and we are determined to continue our efforts to remove possible sources of difference, and thus to contribute to assure the peace of Europe.

(Signed) *Hitler*
Neville Chamberlain

The euphoria was immense. But before we think too hardly of Neville Chamberlain – a thoroughly honourable man – or of those who applauded him, it is as well to ask how later critics would themselves have reacted to the news of a peace agreement, had they been living in 1938. Might they also have joined in the cheering, or at the very least expressed a sigh of relief – while perhaps sparing a prayer for Czechoslovakia, the victim of the deal?

History has provided us with the advantage of seeing in retrospect what Winston Churchill saw all too clearly at the time, expressed in his own press statement: *'The belief that security can be obtained by throwing a small state to the wolves is a fatal delusion.'* Within three years Churchill had become Britain's wartime Prime Minister.

'To prophesy,' runs the ancient Chinese proverb, 'is extremely difficult – especially in regard to the future.' The twentieth century has borne this out with a vengeance, in the numerous unforeseen crises, conflicts, atrocities and disasters, in which a single misjudgment could catapult whole nations into a nightmare without an obvious end – and, in addition, consign innocent optimists into the future ash-heaps of history's heroic failures.

Back in 1938 and 1939, we would not have wished it on anybody, least of all on the German people themselves, to be partnered with Adolf Hitler in a deathly dance of deception! The banal sentiments of the pathetic Munich document are palpable now for their contentlessness – no one today would have any difficulty in estimating the moral value of a scrap of paper signed by Hitler.

Where did the 'piece of paper' end up? How long did a copy of it stay in Chamberlain's desk drawer? Did he look at it from time to time? What have we to learn from that typed scrap of paper, and Chamberlain's innocent trust?

It is, perhaps, a major lesson of all history, and of life upon a fallen world – that human sin and the presence of evil have to be taken seriously. Repeatedly their power is underestimated by the inadequate and self-deceiving world-views that swirl around our civilisation. Over the centuries there have been philosophers, politicians and reformers alike, who have aspired to believe in human nature and to improve it. But as Bernard Levin once declared in *The Times* (16 August 1986), 'Those who plan to sit around until it happens to all mankind had better bring a cushion and a very long book.'

A classic example of stern resolve in the face of weak vacillation is found in Elijah, Israel's outstanding prophet of the ninth century BC. Ahab was the pliable king, and Jezebel his foreign-born Phoenician wife was the subtle influence behind the throne, driving her husband into compromise with the one power that could threaten the peace of the nation. The Canaanites, with their alien worship, were now accommodated within the royal court itself, through 450 of the false prophets of Baal, together with another four hundred prophets of Asherah, the mother-goddess of the Canaanite belief-system.

Ahab is all for the quiet life, and is content to ride along with the dangerous arrangement. It is Elijah who stands obstinately against the blasphemous liaison, and provokes the irritation of his king:

> When he saw Elijah, Ahab said to him, 'Is that you, you troubler of Israel?'
> 'I have not made trouble for Israel,' Elijah replied. 'But you and your father's family have. You have abandoned the LORD's commands and have followed the Baals. Now summon the people from all over Israel to meet me on Mount Carmel. And bring the 450 prophets of Baal and the 400 prophets of Asherah, who eat at Jezebel's table' (1 Kings 18:17-19).

The man of principle is insistent; this wavering of God's people between two alternative theologies has got to stop, for Israel's sake, for the truth's sake, for the sake of God's name and integrity. The time for compromise is over, with Elijah's challenge, *'How long will you waver between two opinions?'*

It is the age-long tension that has been with us from the beginning. We can see it as the issue of:

Principle Against Expedience

It started with Eve, back in Genesis chapter 3. A little flattery from the Devil, and she's won over.

'He's very nice,' she says to Adam. 'I've been having quite a chat with him. He says if only we follow his advice, we can be like God. *I trust Satan.*'

As Billy Graham once wrote, 'Satan's purpose was not to make Eve as ungodly as possible, but to make her as god-like as possible, without God.'[1]

So it is, in the case of Ahab, with his easy-going gullibility and his hope of gaining the best of two worlds. Sure, he would like to worship the true and only God of Israel – but to fit in Baal and Asherah as well. And, with his wife beside him, why – it would help the marriage too! Perhaps, he reasons, there can be more than one 'truth', and some principles are terribly uncomfortable to live with. We don't have to be so strait-laced. *'I....trust Jezebel!'*

It was a perennial deathtrap for Israel. A century later, Hosea the prophet protests that his people are *like a dove, easily deceived and senseless, now calling to Egypt, now turning to Assyria* (Hosea 7:11). They were engaging, as he saw it, against God's will, in useless peace pacts that only blunted Israel's distinctive witness to the nations. *I trust Egypt.*

Principle against expedience. As against that, there is the example of Jesus. In the baking wilderness of temptation, the Devil is pulling out trick after trick:

> *Jesus, you're weak! Have you* really *come to save the world? Don't you realise the world is* mine?....*Look here, I'll make you an offer; we'll be partners. You can change the world. Armies and navies, roads and ships, banks and businesses; ALL YOURS...in exchange for one little bow to me?*

---

1. Billy Graham, *Approaching Hoofbeats,* Word Books, 1983, p. 105.

> But Jesus is firm: *Satan, your power is very great.*
> *But I haven't come to join you. I've come to beat you*
> *...There'll be no short cuts, no cheap tricks, no stunts...*[2]

The final crisis approaches with the death of Jesus. His close disciple, Simon Peter, had tried to discourage him from taking the road to Jerusalem and danger, but Jesus would have none of it. Can we imagine him saying, 'Oh, very well, if you say so; *I trust you, Peter*?' From the start, he was consistent in his attitude:

> Jesus would not entrust himself to them, for he knew all men (John 2:24).

Back in the story of 1 Kings, Elijah is under no illusions. There before him are a people of ditherers. Perhaps some would have claimed that theirs was a broad-minded and strong approach to religious outlook – a fusing together of the God of Israel with Baal and Asherah. How tolerant and open-minded! How mean and narrow of Elijah!

But no – their 'broadmindedness' was what James describes in his New Testament letter as 'double-mindedness...unstable in all its ways'. Frankly, the appeal of such 'toleration' is no more than that of Hinduism with its coalition of gods. With such a world-view, you can believe anything you like. The appropriate question to a traditional Hindu – or a modern New-Ager for that matter – is not 'What do you believe?' but rather *'What do you deny?'*

The ideological contest, staged by Elijah on Mount Carmel some twenty-eight centuries ago, was a battle for the preservation of God's given revelation of himself as the only God. It was a collision of truth against synthesis, as God's prophet ordered two rival altars to be prepared with

---

2. Andrew Knowles, *The Way Out,* Collins, 1977, pp. 27, 28.

a sacrifice. The test was terrifying and unequivocal. It was agreed that prayers would be offered by Elijah and his Canaanite opponents, and *the God who answered* would, from then on, be respected and worshipped as the only God. The consuming by fire of one of the sacrifices would alone constitute a valid 'answer'!

Elijah is indomitable. *'Asherah?'* he exclaims, 'this non-existent fertility queen? *Baal* – this supposed nature god of fire? Then let's meet fire with fire!'

And the contest is on. King Ahab's eyes are popping, for this is an issue that is very personal to him. It is one of *Principle against Expedience*. Once identify this as the crux of the problem – and it is not all that far removed from Chamberlain's accommodation of Adolf Hitler. But there is a second issue to be recognised:

Engagement against Appeasement

The word e*ngagement* is chosen with care, because, in any confrontation – whether political or ideological – *engagement* can take a variety of forms. It does not have to be limited to the raw power of military force. Indeed, when God's people historically have relied upon arms to achieve their objective as a church – as in the days of the Crusades against the Turks – the inevitable result has been an immediate loss of moral and spiritual power.

Israel, for its part, was for ever placing its reliance upon foreign military deals that invariably ended in failure. This is not to make a rigid argument for pacifism in the case of Britain in 1939. The main issue lies in a question: Are we simply to cave in when faced by a power that is unacceptable to our own belief system? The answer must be that in one way or another such a power is to be engaged, resisted and, if possible, overthrown – and supremely with the weapon of Truth. Strength of conviction and cool resolution play the key role when false ideologies are on the rampage.

Alien world-views are not to be appeased, but opposed.
To go back to 1938, with hindsight it can be recognised that the British government seemed to be underestimating what it was up against in the Hitler regime. Neville Chamberlain told the House of Commons that he thought he had established '*some degree of personal influence over Herr Hitler*', and that he was '*satisfied that Herr Hitler would not go back on his word once he had given it*'.

It is tempting to place all the blame on Chamberlain. There were plenty of others willing, like him, to believe the best and to hope that the tensions would be peaceably resolved. It would have been the same in Elijah's day. There would have been those who would have preferred not to see Jezebel's packing of the royal court with false prophets:

'You know these Baal-worshippers; they aren't all that different from us; they're really quite decent people. Some of them are among my best friends.'

'We must try to get *close* to these prophets of Asherah; we must try to *understand* them.'

But to all this, Elijah would have retorted, 'I understand them very well! We're not going to accommodate this idolatry. Come along! Set up the altars. The God who answers by fire – *he* is God. Agreed?'

Faced by this human bulldozer, the Israelites complied, and the sacrifices were prepared. *No compromise.* When for some years I ran a newspaper question-and-answer column, I recall one fascinating question from West Africa. It ran as follows: *We are told to pray for our enemies; so would it not be right to love our enemy the Devil and to pray for his conversion?* My answer had to be in terms of the Scriptures being a book of salvation and belief for *humans* and not for angels, and that there was to be no dialoguing with the Devil, whose fate is in any case already sealed.

No compromise! No parleying when confronted by outright evil and error. Not for a moment does Elijah waver. He exemplifies a policy of engagement, not appeasement, and in this he lays down a marker for future generations of believing people, buffeted and bullied into joining hands with alien beliefs. When this has happened in the church, the result is disarray, a drop in membership and a massive loss of spiritual power, for God makes fools out of those who negotiate with idolatry and error.

But a third issue presents itself:

The Prophetic against the Hysteric

Sometimes the line that separates these two categories seems paper-thin, but it's there all right. It is perfectly highlighted in Elijah's encounter with the false prophets:

> At noon, Elijah began to taunt them. 'Shout louder!' he said. 'Surely he is a god! Perhaps he is deep in thought, or busy, or travelling. Maybe he is sleeping and must be awakened.' So they shouted louder and slashed themselves with swords and spears, as was their custom, until their blood flowed (1 Kings 18: 27–28).

With the hysterics it's all push and shove, noise and chanting – and very human-based. That can never be God's way. As Sören Kierkegaard once put it: *Ten thousand lips, shouting the same thing, makes the statement fraudulent, even if it happens to be true.*

Something of that frenzied atmosphere prevailed on the day when Jesus Christ rode into Jerusalem on the first Palm Sunday, only days before his death. Much of the clamour was unthinking hysteria, surrounding a mistaken view of Messiahship: *He's here at last...the Conquering Hero... Freedom at last from the Roman yoke... Peace in our time!* But, according to prophecy, that never was to be the style of the world's true Messiah. 'He will not shout or cry out, or raise his voice in the streets' (Isa. 42:2).

The prophetic against the hysteric; the prophet Elijah may be the fiery 'troubler of Israel' – but he stays cool, and very confident. He is confident partly because of a fourth issue that is at stake in this dramatic showdown:

Prayer against Inertia

The gulf between the true prophet and the false is huge. Elijah stands for prayer; the false leaders attempt magic. *What is the difference?*

In magic, humans are attempting to exert *control* – to bend unseen forces to become their servant and bring about their desired will. *They* are in the driving seat. Even though religious words and emblems may be used, *they are trying to make it happen,* and in so doing they are plugging in below.

With prayer it is the other way round completely. Essentially, it is *God* who is in the driving seat. In no way is he there as our servant; we are *his* servants, co-operating with his set purposes by prayer – which is his chosen way of involving us in the bringing about of his will. Through the means of prayer he is saying, 'As my servants, *you* pray; *I* will work!' Elijah's prayer shows all too clearly who is in charge and who is the servant!

At the time of sacrifice, the prophet Elijah stepped forward and prayed: 'O LORD, God of Abraham, Isaac and Israel, let it be known today that you are God in Israel and that I am your servant and have done all these things at your command. Answer me, O LORD, answer me, so these people will know that you, O LORD, are God, and that you are turning their hearts back again.' Then the fire of the LORD fell...(1 Kings 18:36-38).

When many people look around at their city, at their country – at the world as it is at this moment – they wonder whether the whole human race is out of control. Is there anything that can be done by anybody, beyond being armchair TV spectators, while whole societies become dismembered before their eyes?

But we don't have to lapse into a passive inertia. Prayer is the most powerful activity we will ever engage in. As Toyohiko Kagawa of Japan once declared, *The world is opened by prayer.* In prayer we may exert as much influence in some distant country as if we were there in person. Elijah turns to God, the only God, the God who *answers,* and the prayer is used to unlock the situation of apathy and compromise that had so gripped the nation...and the fire falls.

One is enough – in a business, a family, a student campus or in a cabinet of political ministers. Actually, in Elijah's case there were more than one; in the following chapter the prophet collapses in reaction after the strain and triumph of Carmel; and he imagines that he is the only faithful believer around. It is then that he is reminded that there were actually seven thousand others who had stayed faithful; *silent,* perhaps, but they were there. It only took one person of conviction and initiative to bring them out of their lethargy and to stop wavering.

On the political front it was Winston Churchill who did that for Britain in the dark days of World War II; who encouraged the waverers and 'provided the roar' of resolution and confidence for the free world. He is joined by such as Alexander Solzhenitsyn, Nelson Mandela, J.F. Kennedy and Martin Luther King.

The new century is beginning with a blank sheet of paper. Whose names will be paramount, for *good* – standing for Principle as against Expedience, Engagement as against Appeasement, the Prophetic as against the Hysteric and Prayer as against Inertia? With the prayer of faith we may believe that they will surface.

One name alone will dominate, and it will be Christ's name. Numerous attempts will be made to suppress it, but they will fail.

The great eighteenth-century Swiss theologian, Johannes Von Muller, wrote some seventeen thousand pages of history – but summed them all up with his significant statement:

> Christ is the key to the history of the world...I marvel not at miracles; a far greater miracle has been reserved for our times, the spectacle of the connection of all human events in the establishment and preservation of the doctrines of Christ.

The twenty-first century began with fireworks and celebrations of hope everywhere. I shall be happy, if I can summon the strength to continue the new millennium sharing a sentiment that will be common to some two billion people: *I trust...Jesus Christ.*

3

'Power grows out of the barrel of a gun'

(Chairman Mao Tse Tung,
6 November 1938)

Did you know that when Alfred Nobel of Sweden introduced dynamite to the world in 1866, he called it *Security Powder*! The idea behind his invention was to promote peace and stability across the world.

'I hope,' he once wrote, 'to discover a weapon so terrible that it would make war eternally impossible.' It is sobering to reflect that the profits from Nobel's inventions were dedicated to what became known as the Nobel Peace Prize.

If Alfred Nobel had understood the biblical doctrine of the Fall a little better, he would have been under no illusions! From the bow and arrow onwards, however dangerous newly invented weapons might be to human life, people and entire nations have had no hesitation about using them – not for 'security', but to promote violence and war. By 1970 a single American nuclear submarine possessed the capacity to destroy 160 Russian cities simultaneously. Despite the deterrent of 'Mutually Assured Destruction' between East and West, the arms race continued its incredible acceleration.

Here was a conflict of Capitalism against Communism; it was an ideological contest. But are convictions and thought forms to be overcome by force of arms? Professor Bob Goudzwaard of Amsterdam thinks not:

> A little reflection shows that ideologies can be fought only with spiritual weapons. A military attack calls for a military defense, but an advancing ideology requires a spiritual defense. It is therefore a mistake, and a fruit of ideological thinking, to exacerbate existing military tensions in the world for the sake of fighting an ideology. Then deploying every military means is fully legitimated by the desire to battle *a demon*...

Against that demon, we permit ourselves the most hideous means of destruction. But have we not fallen prey to an ideology equally as totalitarian as communism?[1]

This was the fallacy lying behind the Crusades of eight and nine hundred years ago. It spells out the ultimate death knell facing every *jihad* or holy war between religious groups today. You are simply not going to capture the mindsets and loyalties of great numbers of people by force. It is amazing that no totalitarian regime or authoritarian religious body has learnt this yet. One by one, each ends up in the dustbowl of extinct belief systems and vanished empires.

For this reason the quotation from Mao Tse Tung that heads this chapter was archaic even as it was being written. Born the son of a peasant farmer, Mao rose to become the first chairman of the Chinese People's Republic in 1949. Earlier he had urged, 'Every Communist must grasp the truth, **"Political power grows out of the barrel of a gun"**.' Mao expands thus:

Experience in the class struggle in the era of imperialism teaches us that it is only by the power of the gun that the working class and the labouring masses can defeat the armed bourgeoisie and landlords; in this sense we may say that only with guns can the whole world be transformed.[2]

1. Bob Goudzwaard, *Idols of our Time,* IVP, 1981, p. 74.
2. *Problems of War and Strategy,* 1938, p. 224.

It remains to be seen how far into the twenty-first century this Maoist teaching can keep running! From the Babylonian, Greek and Roman empires through to present-day tyrannies, we have come to recognise that every apparatus of state dedicated to keeping a people docile and obedient to a doctrinaire system has a limited life-span. *These monoliths cannot last.* There is something about the human spirit that knows when it is being crushed down, and eventually finds the will to resist.

As against these oppressors, there is another kingdom that has been steadily growing for thousands of years. It boasts no armies or navies; it runs no banks or businesses; it is not confined to any one country or area of the globe. It is universal and it is permanent. *It is the kingdom of God,* the rule of the one and only God, through Jesus Christ the chosen King, in the lives of his subjects everywhere, hundreds of millions of them. By grace I am a member of this kingdom. Are you yet?

Power grows out of the barrel of a gun. The lie takes a long time dying!

Such a statement must always reckon with the kingdom which will outlast all others. To read the prophecy given to John, writing as an exiled apostle of Jesus Christ, is to discover that there is an alternative interpretation of 'power' and its true source:

And I will give power to my two witnesses, and they will prophesy for 1,260 days, clothed in sackcloth. These are the two olive trees and the two lampstands that stand before the Lord of the earth. If anyone tries to harm them, fire comes from their mouths and devours their enemies. This is how anyone who wants to harm them must die. These men have power

to shut up the sky so that it will not rain during the
time they are prophesying; and they have power to
turn the waters into blood and to strike the earth
with every kind of plague as often as they want (Rev.
11:3-6).

We will come on later to the identity of the 'two witnesses'.
But for the present, here is John the beloved evangelist –
himself the victim of first-century Roman violence – isolated
on Patmos, a small island off what is now the Turkish coast.
It is there that he receives the dramatic apocalyptic vision
from Christ, risen, ascended and glorified. It is the vision
that rounds off the Scriptures in a burst of inspired prophecy.
The book of Revelation has comforted believers in Jesus
Christ from the time of the imperial dictator, Titus Flavius
Domitian, through to today's rampaging fundamentalisms
of all brands, political and religious. There have always been
such oppressors – razing villages to the ground, setting places
of worship alight and driving citizens from their homes by
the tens of thousands.

   In this prophecy, awesome and riveting, John has set
out for his readers, first, seven 'letters' from Christ in glory
to certain selected churches, bringing them messages
containing comfort, praise, rebuke and challenge. The vision
switches in chapters 4 and 5 to the throne of God and the
Lamb of God – the ultimate centre and explanation of all
our life on earth. This is followed by the seven seals and
then the seven trumpets – a spectacular panoramic spread
of the patterns in history that may be expected both by the
church and by a rebel world under judgment (the plagues,
the wars, the calamities and persecutions) and through them
all, the preservation and advance of the church.

Here in our passage, we are in-between the sixth and seventh trumpets, with these chapters 10 and 11 coming as a kind of interlude of reassurance for the people of God. In chapter 10, John receives a 'scroll' of commissioning from the angelic messenger. In chapter 11, we are presented with an unfolding of expectations in the face of a world that refuses to repent at the warning judgments of history – turning its wrath and power on the church. But then comes the surprise!

And I will give power to my two witnesses...These men have power to shut up the sky...to turn the waters into blood.

Divine 'power' of this kind is surely the only kind worth having. The passage in Revelation bears a strong link with the Old Testament prophet Zechariah and chapter 4 – where God's message is given to the prophet after a period of national disaster, faced now by the urgent task of Jewish reconstruction. How was God's servant to succeed? Zechariah 4:6 spells out the principle: **'Not by might, nor by power, but by my Spirit,' says the LORD Almighty.**

Here are principles that carry down through all history, for those who have eyes to see them, and a willingness to be teachable.

Ideas are sharper than swords. Think of Moses and the deliverance of the Israelites from Egyptian might, or of Gideon and his three hundred men – the 'few' against the many – or of David the unknown herdboy against the Philistine giant, Goliath. I am not making out a case for pacifism here, but rather contending that the world is changed not by the war machine so much as by the power of an idea.

Spirit is superior to flesh. I can think of Corrie Ten Boom of Holland, whose shining faith during World War II carried her through intense adversity. 'Love is larger than the walls that shut it in,' she later confided. I think too of the Ugandan evangelist-bishop, Festo Kivengere. Hounded out of his own diocese during Idi Amin's terror campaign of the mid-1970s, Festo was asked by a reporter in New York what he would do if he was sitting in a chair opposite the dictator, and had a gun at his side. 'I would hand the gun to President Amin,' replied the bishop, 'and say to him, "This is not my weapon. I think it must be yours. My weapon is love".'

Good is stronger than evil. There is a permanence about goodness that evil can never share. Good and evil are not parallel and equal forces running side by side in eternal conflict; there is no dualism in Christian thinking. God and goodness belong to eternity, whereas evil has entered as an interruption, and will be brought to a definite end at the close of the age when Christ returns to consummate the victory won over evil at the Cross. When the kingdom of darkness is finally destroyed, there will be no comeback! Goodness and love will reign supreme for ever.

These are the convictions that have given the church its confidence as it has witnessed and suffered across the ages. As the sixteenth-century French scholar Theodore Beza once commented to his king, 'Sire, it belongs to the Church of Christ, for which I speak, to receive blows rather than to deal them; but your Majesty will remember that it is an anvil which has worn out many hammers.' The twentieth century, more than any preceding era, has been marked by the persecution and killing of Christian believers by the million, in numerous countries – but the church continues inexorably to grow, despite its appearance of weakness. How to explain its resilience, its *power*?

Back to the 'two witnesses' and to Revelation chapter 11. Here we see four facets of the church that are typical from earliest times down to the present day:

The squeezing of the church

In Revelation 11:1-2, the evangelist is told to go and 'measure' – or *sanctify* – the temple of God, distinguishing carefully between its sanctuary and its outer courts. The language is borrowed from Ezekiel 42:20. Those within the sanctuary are numbered; they are the *insiders,* and they are safe. They are God's own people. But the outer courts are vulnerable; they are for the peripheral, the careless, the nominal believers. Oppression sets in as the unbelieving world, represented by 'the Gentiles', takes over this area and proceeds to trample down the holy city for forty-two months.

The real church is safe. This does not mean that there are no casualties and martyrdoms; there are. But Christ's own people remain intact throughout this period of adversity. This is what we are to expect throughout our Christian era. We were promised no less from our founder – oppression, but throughout, his own divine and permanent security:

> In this world you will have trouble. But take heart! I have overcome the world (John 16:33).

But hand in hand with this portrayal of the church, and simultaneous with it, is a second historical facet:

The spreading of the church

Revelation 11:3-6 introduces the enigmatic 'two witnesses'. The clue to their identity lies in their actions – they have power to shut up the sky and to turn waters into blood (v.6).

Why, of course! One is Elijah, who pronounced drought upon the land that would last for three and a half years (forty-two months); and the other must be Moses, who pronounced a series of plagues upon Egypt – including the turning of the waters of the Nile into blood. *Elijah,* the most prominent of all the Old Testament prophets, and *Moses,* the great lawgiver of the Old Testament people of God.

The law and the prophets. *These* are the two witnesses, symbolising the powerful mission and outreach of the church at times of great oppression. Here are clear tokens of authority, reinforced by mention of the two olive trees and lampstands of verse 4. The olive trees and lampstands refer back to the Old Testament, to Zechariah 4:11-14, where they are identified as *missionary* representatives – 'These are the two who are anointed to serve the Lord of all the earth.' Perhaps there is an intended allusion here to the product of the olive tree, oil being a symbol of the Holy Spirit, and also used in anointing for special service.

This passage, then, of the two witnesses portrays a period of great *ascendancy and power* for God's people – lasting for how long? 1,260 days. Why...that is identical in time to the forty-two months of the *oppression* mentioned in the previous verse. It is precisely equivalent to the *three and a half years* of Elijah's stopping of the rain!

> Elijah was a man just like us. He prayed earnestly that it would not rain, and it did not rain on the land for three and a half years (James 5:17).

It comes together now. Elijah's period out in the wilderness was one of intense opposition for the people of God, but it was also a time of unparalleled influence and power. *This three and a half year period for Elijah is taken in the book of*

Revelation to symbolise the **advance through adversity** *of our entire Christian era.* When we pray we may expect results, however great the pressures; when we proclaim the good news of Christ in the power and energy of the Holy Spirit, we may look for things to happen! Down to our present day we can say that we are in the testing but powerful period of the 'two witnesses'! Ever since Christ's first coming, we have experienced fierce opposition, but it has been matched by the spreading of the church.

A third facet:

The silencing of the church

The evangelist portrays a grim episode in which it appears that the enemies of the church have finally won the battle:

> Now when they have finished their testimony, the beast that comes up from the Abyss will attack them, and overpower and kill them. Their bodies will lie in the street of the great city, which is figuratively called Sodom and Egypt, where also their Lord was crucified. For three and a half days men from every people, tribe, language and nation will gaze on their bodies and refuse them burial. The inhabitants of the earth will gloat over them and will celebrate by sending each other gifts, because these two prophets had tormented those who live on earth (Rev. 11:7-10).

Is this futuristic? The answer is 'Yes' and 'No'. 'No', because we have frequently witnessed in history this phenomenon of the church's apparent destruction, much to the joy of its enemies. Why, the Roman emperor Diocletian even had a special medal struck in the third century AD to celebrate the demise of the church! Little did he know that the day would come when the church would stand over the grave of the empire he represented.

But yes, this passage indeed possesses a futuristic element in the rise and apparent victory of 'the beast' – the persecutor of the church who is portrayed in Revelation 13 as rising against the church at the End Times.

The pattern of the prophecy reveals that when the period of Christian witness has been completed, there will be a short period (only three and a half days, as compared with the three and a half years of verse 3) during which the church's voice will appear to have been silenced. Wickedness (Sodom and Egypt) will seem to have triumphed conclusively. No longer will people's consciences be troubled by the two witnesses; the celebrations will begin. The church is dead! God is dead! But then comes the turning of the tables:

The rising of the church

The defeat of the church is short-lived. It is heaven that has the last word, as God acts on behalf of his own, in stupendous and vindicating power:

> But after the three and a half days a breath of life from God entered them, and they stood on their feet, and terror struck those who saw them. Then they heard a loud voice from heaven saying to them, 'Come up here.' And they went up to heaven in a cloud, while their enemies looked on (Rev. 11:11– 12).

Again and again the book of Revelation reminds its readers of the victory theme – victory over evil, won initially at the Cross of Jesus Christ, and then sealed eternally with his triumphant return. It is the theme of the winning goal – filmed on the video repeatedly from different camera positions. At the end of time, events will force even the bitterest of Christ's enemies to concede, however grudgingly, his power and victory.

It is said that the cat has nine lives. The church has infinitely more! Squeezed and hemmed in across the centuries, it possesses nonetheless a power and influence in the lives of millions of people. Threatened with extinction on numerous occasions, it continues to rise again.

Power grows out of the barrel of a gun.

The history of the human race, coupled with the testimony of Christ's community and the voice of God's book, come back with their own riposte; *Terribly sorry, it ain't true.*

4

'I have a dream'

(Martin Luther King,
28 August 1963)

History is just about the most thrilling subject in the world...but it took me a long time to fall in love with it. Perhaps I was unlucky with my teachers at school. Whatever the period – King Alfred, the Battle of Agincourt, Cromwell or the Boston Tea Party – my mentors could be guaranteed to strip from the action all imagination, colour and movement, and reduce the adventure of our civilisation to a weary, grey calendar of yawning tedium. But there is no mistaking the real thing.

'History is made by imagination,' wrote the historian T.R. Glover. 'No man creates till his own imagination is touched, and till he touches the imagination of his fellows.'

Such a man was the Rev. Martin Luther King.

There were 210,000 people waiting for the black Civil Rights leader that Sunday morning by the Lincoln Memorial. It was exactly a hundred years after Abraham Lincoln's momentous announcement of emancipation for every slave in America, and the speaker had chosen his moment well. 'We have come to our nation's capital,' he cried, *'to cash a check!'*

It was also significant that the steps of the Lincoln Memorial, from which King spoke, had been the site selected some years earlier by Eleanor Roosevelt, for the performance of songs by a black singer whom she was supporting. Her action then had been in protest against the refusal of her protégé's performance by the nearby Opera House. This was on account of the singer's colour.

Imagination, drama and fever-pitch resolution were converging, then, on a day in history – 28 August 1963 – as the vast audience watched the magic settle on their spokesman. He was only thirty-four, born in Atlanta, Georgia, the son of a Baptist pastor. Already he had reached national prominence as leader of the Alabama bus boycott.

Now, at the end of the march he had led on Washington, he was ready with his speech. He had finished preparing it at four o'clock that morning.

> I have a dream that my four little children will one day live in a nation where they will not be judged by the color of their skin, but by the content of their character.
> I have a dream today.
> I have a dream that one day the state of Alabama, whose governor's lips are presently dripping with the words of interposition and nullification, will be transformed into a situation where little black boys and black girls will be able to join hands with little white boys and white girls and walk together as sisters and brothers.
> I have a dream today.

*I have a dream...*It was, by wide acclaim, the political speech of the twentieth century; a speech that will endure for always. In it, King outlawed violence as a pathway to civil rights, inspiring his listeners instead to 'rise to the majestic heights of meeting physical force with soul force'.

Within months, Martin Luther King was *Time* magazine's 'Man of the Year', and in 1964 he was awarded the Nobel Peace Prize. Civil Rights Acts were carried through Congress in 1964 and 1965. And on Thursday, 4 April 1968, King was assassinated. The whole civilised world seemed to shake with his passing.

I have a dream. It is this kind of visionary feel for history, for the big landmarks, that draws its inspiration from the gigantic world-view of the Bible. Martin Luther King's speech drew generously from its thought-forms and language:

> I have a dream that one day every valley shall be
> exalted, every hill and mountain shall be made low,
> the rough places will be made plains, and the crooked
> places will be made straight, and the glory of the Lord
> shall be revealed, and all flesh shall see it together.

Such language, with its vision of healing and unity between peoples and of ultimate universal accord, is the language of Isaiah and the prophets; it is the language of eschatology and the last things; it is language that expresses a belief in the sweep and destiny of all history. It is the way of interpreting life and the future *that inspires action in the present.*

The visitor to London, England should pause at the capital's centre, Piccadilly Circus, where the statue of Eros was erected in commemoration of the great Christian philanthropist, Ashley Cooper, the seventh Earl of Shaftesbury. Known two hundred years ago as 'The Poor Man's Earl', he worked tirelessly in Parliament and through the institutions to bring about better conditions for workers, for children and the disadvantaged. Always it was his confidence that the future belonged to Christ and the church that fired his public service:

> I do not think that in the last forty years I have lived
> one conscious hour that was not influenced by the
> thought of our Lord's return.

It is the old principle of a person's view of the *final* day giving depth and meaning to the actions of *every* day. If you have an inadequate grasp of the future, be sure that the present will not make much sense at all! The toil and frustrations facing all campaigners for civil and religious liberty will exact such a toll, that the enterprise would run into the ground, but for the final vision that inspires all lasting reforms. This vision finds expression in the last chapter of the Bible:

> Then the angel showed me the river of the water of life, as clear as crystal, flowing from the throne of God and of the Lamb down the middle of the great street of the city. On each side of the river stood the tree of life, bearing twelve crops of fruit, yielding its fruit every month. And the leaves of the tree are for the healing of the nations.
>
> No longer will there be any curse. The throne of God and of the Lamb will be in the city, and his servants will serve him. They will see his face, and his name will be on their foreheads. There will be no more night. They will not need the light of a lamp or the light of the sun, for the Lord God will give them light. And they will reign for ever and ever (Rev. 22:1-5).

*The healing of the nations...*In this, the concluding prophecy of a great kaleidoscope of visions, the apostle John writes from his enforced exile on the island of Patmos. With luminous clarity he visualises the ultimate scene that awaits him and the whole of Christ's believing community on earth. It is of a garden city, and its very images speak of beauty and purity, of refreshment, worship, health, and control; of universal understanding and *unity* – the very qualities yearned for in that historic meeting with Martin Luther King in 1963.

It was around AD 95 when John's prophecy was received. No President Kennedy or Johnston, then, but the 44-year-old Roman emperor Domitian, who a year later would be assassinated. By force he governed a vast domain that was served by some sixty million slaves, who faced no living possibility of emancipation. The Christian church within the Roman empire was for the most part composed of slaves. It is with this readership in mind, together with the harassed church of all the ages, that John shares his dream-like vision – and not just of what *can* be (as in Luther King's speech), but of what *will* be!

The final vision! As the reader comes to these last pages of the Bible, there is a sensation of walking into a cinema at the precise moment when the feature film is just ending. Only five minutes have to elapse before the next showing begins. You can have the experience, then, of seeing both ends of the same film rather close together!

That is my own impression of Revelation 21 and 22. It is as though I have taken up my Bible, and bent the back of it *around,* to make the last page meet the first! In a remarkable and divinely inspired way the Bible – over the long sixteen centuries during which it was written – concludes with such astonishing unity of thought, that the end can be said to have met the beginning again. It could never have been contrived like this.

John's battered, squeezed and enslaved readers were, by this dream and vision, lifted out of themselves and given, in these glowing chapters, a unified rationale for living and overcoming. Here was a credible world-view that would enable them, in and through the church, to outlive and outlast the Roman galleys, the enforced labour, the power-mad Caesars and the ten major persecutions that would be launched against them in their first three centuries of witness.

The end meets the beginning. The entire Bible story holds together in a unity. Life and existence – in Christ and his church – *do* make sense, even when you possess neither citizenship nor voting rights. It is this conviction that has marked all the world's great reformers – Florence Nightingale, Ashley Cooper, William Wilberforce, Luther King and Nelson Mandela. It is a confidence in the big picture; that – despite all our earthly confusions – the end meets the beginning in a cohesive whole. Life on this world *does* hold together – first in what I call:

The two creations

Again we must emphasise that the unity between the Bible's beginning and end could never have been planned. Here is the first sentence in the Old Testament:

> In the beginning God created the heavens and the earth (Gen. 1:1).

Compare this with the apostle John:

> Then I saw a *new* heaven and a *new* earth, for the first heaven and the first earth had passed away (Rev. 21:1).

It is, then, as we come to the final vision that we can perceive how the end has met the beginning, with reference to the two creations, the old and the new. And it is this expectation of the new that puts fresh heart into those who fight against the evils of the old order. Jesus referred to '*the renewal of all things, when the Son of Man sits on his glorious throne*' (Matthew 19:28). The phrase 'renewal of all things' is translated from a single Greek word, *palingeneseia* – literally, *the new Genesis*. As the commentators put it, 'the first chapter of the Bible describes God *making* the world; the last chapter shows him *remaking* it.'

Again, we can observe the reference, back in Genesis 2, to the tree of life and the tree of the knowledge of good and evil (v.9). Verse 10 tells us of a river, watering the garden and flowing from Eden. By the time we get to Revelation 22, it is just one tree (v.2) – but what a tree! It stands, we learn, 'on each side of the river', providing a never-ending supply for all who are given access – with its very leaves giving healing to the nations.

As for the river, it flows, crystal pure (v.1) – but now, not out of Eden, but from the divine throne, occupied jointly by God and the Lamb. The underlying emphasis is of purity, of plenty – and perhaps especially of *unity*. It is *one* tree, not two; and *one* river, no longer divided, as in Genesis.

Foundational to the vision is the prophecy of Ezekiel 47:12, in which a river is pictured, flowing out of God's temple, spanned with trees. This is clearly fulfilled in Revelation's final scene. *Is this YOUR projected final scene?* How would you describe your own view of the End Times? The channelling of your energies, your ethics and value system, all that you stand and live for, are vitally affected by your concept of the future.

In his book on England, covering the years 1870-1914, the radical historian R.C.K. Ensor commented that no one will understand nineteenth-century England if they fail to understand its evangelical influence – particularly as exercised by the reforming group based at Holy Trinity Church, Clapham. They were known as The Clapham Sect:

If one asks how nineteenth century English merchants earned the reputation of being the most honest in the world (a very real factor in the prominence of English trade), the answer is: Because hell and heaven seemed as certain to them as tomorrow's sunrise and the Last Judgment as real as the week's balance sheet.[1]

Ensor goes on to write that the other side of this moral accountancy was the belief that this life is only important as a preparation for the next, for evangelicalism made 'other-worldliness' an everyday conviction and inspired a highly civilised people to put duty before all else.

The knowledge that the old creation is to be transformed into the new is enough to rejuvenate every generation that feels tired and weighed down by this present, dying world. The end will meet the beginning again, as we see in the two creations. But in John's final curtain call I discern something else:

The two Testaments

And the leaves of the tree are for the healing of the nations. From the start, God had all the nations in view. He said as much to Abraham, in the initial establishing of the divinely contracted covenant:

> And all peoples on earth will be blessed through you ...I have made you a father of many nations (Gen. 12:3; 17:5).

Israel, to be sure, was to be the lamp-standard to the nations, but ultimately it is Jesus, in the new covenant and the gospel, who – as the sacrificial Lamb of God – completes God's mission to the nations, at the Cross. It is for this reason that 'the Lamb' features so prominently at the Bible's close. It is because of him – the figure who spans both the Old

---

1. R.C.K. Ensor, *England, 1870-1914*, 1936, p. 137.

and New Testaments – that Eden comes to be restored, and sin abolished entirely: *No longer will there be any curse* (Rev. 22:3).

In this wonderful last chapter, the evangelist is saying, *I have a dream*. It is a vision which will 'soon' be implemented. The tree is back! The curse is gone! Men and women are back in communion in the garden city of God! The end has met the beginning again, in the two Testaments, old and new. We bend the last page of the Bible back to meet the first – and Moses and John grasp hands across the centuries. They are combined now in the *one* united testimony to the truth of the Bible.

But now for a third facet:

The two humanities

And his servants will serve him. They will see his face, and his name will be on their foreheads...They will reign for ever and ever (Rev. 22:3-5).

Here is a wonderful combination of ideas within a single paragraph. God's servants in the new order will 'serve' him. But they will also 'reign' for ever and ever. The word *serve* is that used for a bondman, a slave. And yet there is a difference. Here, in the future perfected order, is not a service of oppression, but of *royalty*. God's redeemed people will be King Slaves, Queen Slaves! We may think of it as a future 'dream' – but the members of God's kingdom should be anticipating such service *now,* in the fellowship of the Christian church.

It is this that lies behind Martin Luther King's inspired leadership:

This is our hope. This is the faith with which I return to the South. With this faith we will be able to hew out of the mountain of despair a stone of hope. With this faith we will be able to transform the jangling discords of our nation into a beautiful symphony of brotherhood.

King's words carry echoes of the harmony described by the apostle Paul – the reconciliation of the outsiders with the insiders. It is more than a vision or dream. It is because of the Cross of Christ that Paul can proclaim reconciliation as an historic achievement:

He came and preached peace to you who were far away and peace to those who were near. For through him we both have access to the Father by one Spirit (Eph. 2:17, 18).

It is possible that Martin Luther King, as a preacher himself, had the words of Galatians 3:28 in mind, as he spoke of alienated communities joining hands: 'There is neither Jew nor Greek, slave nor free, male nor female, for you are all one in Christ Jesus.'

The healing of the nations is symbolised by that tree of life in Revelation 22. The New Testament declares it as a present reality – reducing all our cultural or idiosyncratic differences to little more than blips. Christ is the great unifier of humanity. When Richard Chartres, then Bishop of London, visited us in July 1999 at our London church of All Souls, he described the congregation as 'one great United Nations!'

Sometimes the cry goes up: 'Why can't we reconcile all the traditions and cultures within a single universal religion, and so have the best of everything in one system?' The answer is that *it has already been done, in a single person*. 'For God was pleased...through him (Christ) to reconcile to himself all things, whether things on earth or things in heaven, by making peace through his blood, shed on the cross' (Col. 1:19–20).

This is already a reality in our world. Certainly, it is far from perfect. It is all too easy for believers to stray back into a world where the dividing walls go up again. We should insist within our fellowships, worldwide, that the barriers are kept down, and that such unity between divided humanity must be firmly practised in a grand rehearsal of the new order. It is not that ethnic or cultural diversities are done away with by Christ; it is that we are united by something *bigger*. The day of Pentecost was definitive in this respect, as the gospel was preached and the listeners understood, even in their own languages, the wonderful works of God. It was a projection of what was to be!

> Babel is reversed
> The curse is lifted
> Eden is restored
> The tree is returned
> The gates are open

By the time of the end, the tree is standing for open access and welcome. No longer is it guarded by the angels of Genesis, with their flaming swords flashing back and forth. The way is open.

But to whom is it open? It is spelt out for us in terms of glowing hope:

> Blessed are those who wash their robes, that they may have the right to the tree of life and may go through the gates into the city (Rev. 22:14).

Their robes...What are these 'robes' that need to be purified? Why, they are the things you clothe yourself with – the real you that is comprised of attitudes, habits, outlook...the entire system of values acquired over a lifetime. In short, *your robe is your character.*

And how or where is it to be 'washed'? The answer has been given earlier:

> These are they who have come out of the great tribulation; they have washed their robes and made them white in the blood of the Lamb (Rev. 7:14).

I have a dream...

Civilisation owes a salute to those men and women who have entertained a vision on behalf of their fellows, and then have bent their energies to fulfilling the dream. In our Christian understanding, it is – in its best interpretation – a *connected* dream. It is connected to a man called Jesus, who died in humiliating agony on what the Bible calls a *Xulon,* a 'wood'.

But the tree of life here in Revelation 22 is termed by the same word. It, too, is a *Xulon*. Here then is a fourth theme of John's final picture:

The two trees

There are two trees, and one opens the way to the other. Here is the apostle Peter:

> He himself bore our sins in his body on the tree, so that we might die to sins and live for righteousness; by his wounds you have been healed (1 Pet. 2:24).

The tree of the Cross opens the way to the tree of life. We can look backwards to the Cross, and forwards to the tree of life, whose leaves are for the healing of the nations, your healing! Hold on to that message. It makes the difference to everything. The garden city...the tree of life...the throne of God – are you heading that way?

The signposts are clear in John's vision – of the two creations (the old and the new), the two Testaments (Moses touching hands with John), the two humanities (the outsiders reconciled with the insiders), and the two trees, one leading to the other.

'I have a dream.' Do we? It is vital that we do, for it is the vision of what must be that colours all present energies and plans, and puts shape and substance into them. Without a sense of future and direction, life can only strip us of what the old hymn called the *solid joys and lasting treasure that none but Zion's children know.*

5

'I've been on a calendar,
but never on time'

(Marilyn Monroe, 1950)

Despite being something of a last-minuter, I managed to keep my weekly question-and-answer newspaper column going for a full fifteen years. The trick was to disbelieve the editor when he asked for my copy by the Wednesday. I reasoned that every true editor keeps a day or two in hand. At one point he was so alarmed by the fineness of my safety margin that he invited me to send him in a 'spare' column, to be used only in dire emergencies. It was a fine idea, but I blew the precious spare, first time off! We didn't try that one again.

Over the issue of tight deadlines, I have a small affinity with Marilyn Monroe; her reputation was a byword in this regard. It was after her appearance on a calendar in 1950 – for which she was paid $50 – that the twentieth-century goddess of film and fashion was asked whether she had ever been in *Time* magazine. She gave her ambiguously memorable reply, *'I've been on a calendar, but never on Time.'*

There were only a very few individuals of the twentieth century who were universally identified by their first name alone – Elvis...Diana...and ahead of them in sheer staying power, *Marilyn*. Even in recent times her image has featured on advertisements in the London Underground, for such selling points as air-conditioning units (with caption, *Some like it cool*), and low-cost flights to Ireland.

Perhaps the most famous twentieth-century icon of all, Marilyn was everywhere, but nowhere. She never knew for sure who her real father was. A possible candidate was C. Stanley Gifford, a man who offered Marilyn's mother financial help, but refused to have anything to do with the baby.

Thus the baby had no daddy of her own. She was born on 1 June 1926, and the name on her birth certificate was 'Norma Jean Baker'. Her mother Gladys married twice, but neither man was the father of Norma Jean. When Gladys was finally committed to a mental institution, Norma Jean had to spend her infancy and childhood in a series of foster homes in Los Angeles, belonging nowhere, and perpetually uncertain of her own true identity.

She married James Edward Dougherty at sixteen; later she married the great baseball star Joe Di Maggio, and later still Arthur Miller. Although her girlish dream of getting into movies materialised and she was catapulted into world fame as Marilyn Monroe, stability and permanence were to elude her all her short life. She died from an overdose of barbiturates in August 1962 at the age of thirty-six.

It's too easy to place world celebrities into neat categories after their departure, to accept the pronouncements of TV studio experts, or to swallow wild rumours and conspiracy theories bounced around the Internet. Marilyn – as no one before or after her – became a commodity of the twentieth century, and for this reason care has to be taken over any real attempt to define her life, lest the identity of this beautiful, fragile person is simply buried as a sex symbol, only to be exhumed at intervals convenient to consumer and image-making forces.

If her life, and the century she represented, could possibly be interpreted by a piece of Scripture, the Old Testament book of Ecclesiastes is relevant in its portrayal of the meaninglessness that has characterised the last hundred years. This remarkable book gives profile to the 'vanity' of life, once God is removed from view.

> 'Meaningless! Meaningless!' says the Teacher. 'Utterly meaningless! Everything is meaningless' (Eccl. 1:2).

The book of Ecclesiastes could have been written for the twentieth century, in its exposition of the empty life. Certainly the Christian Gospel has taken a firm hold upon our civilisation – but you have only to take a walk along Oxford Street, the Champs Elysée, Kenyatta Avenue or Sunset Boulevard, to see what the twentieth century did to people as yet untouched by the faith of Christ. Marilyn speaks to us in exactly the same terms as 'the Teacher'.

Every baby needs a da-da-Daddy, she sang, back in the fifties. She sang of the traveller *on the River of No Return* – swept on, as she put it, *for ever to be lost in the stormy sea.*

Compare Marilyn's lyrics with those of Ecclesiastes:

Marilyn:

You're always wishing and wanting for...
Something;
When you get what you want,
You don't want what you get...
After you get what you want,
You don't want what you wanted at all.

Ecclesiastes 2:10–11

I denied myself nothing my eyes desired;
I refused my heart no pleasure.
My heart took delight in all my work...
Yet when I surveyed all that
my hands had done
and what I had toiled to achieve,
everything was meaningless,
a chasing after the wind;
nothing was gained under the sun.

The book of Ecclesiastes derives, as its opening sentence declares, from the 'son of David, king of Jerusalem'. Solomon reigned for forty fabulous years in the tenth century BC. His words present us with an inspired critique of life that has become secularised and devoid of faith in God.

Readers have reacted in various ways to the book. Some have romanticised its third chapter and turned it into songs: *For everything there is a season, and a time for every purpose under heaven.* The superficial interpretation would be, 'How attractive; we must write a song on this theme...*a time to be born, and a time to die; a time to plant, and a time to uproot...*

Indeed we would like to think that there was a pattern to nature and to life; *a time to weep, and a time to laugh*; it feels like a rhythm of security. However, if we are a little more perceptive we can discern that the philosopher, or Teacher, as Solomon styles himself, is portraying a different, a deliberately cynical view of things.

> The race is not to the swift
> or the battle to the strong,
> nor does food come to the wise
> or wealth to the brilliant
> or favour to the learned;
> but time and chance
> happen to them all (9:11).

By means of this cynical approach, the Teacher is prodding and pushing his contemporaries into *thinking*. He is goading readers of every age into asking questions. For when people begin to ask questions, there is hope for them!

A time to be born and a time to die..and behind this catalogue of seasons and activities is the lurking question, 'Are we being made to dance to a tune?' As Marilyn Monroe once perceptively put it, 'Hollywood is a place where they'll pay you a thousand dollars for a kiss, and fifty cents for your soul.'

In Ecclesiastes, the Teacher is using cynicism to wake people up! He follows the materialist and the cynic along the lines of their own reasoning. He's pushing his readers along their own logical pathways; he bends himself deliberately in their direction – towards emptiness and despair.

Michael Hews, in the Scripture Union *Viewpoint* magazine (No. 38), has written in similar vein of the hollow 'freedoms' pursued by so many:

> Free! To sleep, rise, eat, work, eat,
>   work, watch, sleep, rise;
> Free to grow older, older,
>   Free to retire.
> Free to weed our gardens,
>   Free to grow older still
> – and shakily water our window-boxes.
> Free to die – and get our names in the
>   local papers for just one more time.
> Free to live, to die, to be forgotten;
> We who have lived all of our lives
>   in the slavery of the fear of death,
> and the fear of life without meaning.

A closer look at the book of Ecclesiastes enables the reader to identify several cameos of the empty life in its opening chapters:

Chapter 1: Identity eroded by the ceaseless cycle

Life is perceived, first of all, as the frustration of travelling endlessly in circles. You are travelling, but getting nowhere:

Generations come and generations go, but the earth remains for ever. The sun rises and the sun sets, and hurries back to where it rises. The wind blows to the south and turns to the north; round and round it goes...What has been will be again, what has been done will be done again; there is nothing new under the sun... (Eccl. 1:4-6, 9).

The celebrated American playwright, Tennessee Williams, summed up the mood of his generation vividly: *What else are we offered? The never-broken procession of little events that assure us that we and strangers about us are still going on? Where? Why? And the perch that we hold is unstable!*
Many are assailed by the question: In one hundred years' time, what evidence will there be that I ever existed?

There is no remembrance of men of old, and even those who are yet to come will not be remembered by those who follow (Eccl. 1:11).

Identity eroded. Marilyn Monroe was the public face of millions of people who have never been able to answer the question of their own personhood. Who am I? What am I? But there is a second cameo here:

Chapter 2: Energy wasted by the aimless life

Solomon, the king who had the world at his feet and could satisfy every passing whim, is in his element throughout chapter 2. He has a try at everything: *The pleasure trip* (v.3) 'I tried cheering myself with wine...' *The business deal* (vv.4-8) 'I undertook great projects...I built houses....I planted vineyards, I made gardens and parks... bought male and female slaves....I amassed silver and gold for myself...' *The study course* (vv.12-14) 'Then I turned my thoughts to consider wisdom...'

In all this, what is missing? *It is the lack of any obvious centre and any significant relationships.* Before she went to New York, Marilyn Monroe admitted, 'I never had any friends, only conquests. I didn't have the time to find real friends. I was always being looked at; I had no chance to look.'

Not that Marilyn was without the capacity for affection. The indication from her two failed pregnancies and one miscarriage is that she loved children and longed to have had them. There is no solid evidence for the stories of numerous abortions that pursued her. Nevertheless, the crucial question remains to face everyone looking for fulfilment – whether Solomon, Marilyn Monroe or the children of the new century ahead of us: *Where is the centre, the focus point?*

The Teacher is teasing and tantalising the reader with the elusive goal of success. When the summit has already been gained, what then? *'What more can the king's successor do than what has already been done?'* As Dean Inge of St Paul's Cathedral in London put it many years ago, 'Nothing fails like success.' Further back still, Theophan the Recluse declared, 'Most people are like a shaving of wood which is curled round its central emptiness.'

Identity eroded; energy wasted. But the Teacher has a third cameo waiting for us in chapter 3:

Chapter 3: Eternity blocked by the full agenda

The much-romanticised *A time to be born and a time to die* passage isn't romantic so much as robotic. Chapter 3, in contrast to the first chapter, presents life without God not as a ceaseless cycle but rather as a backwards and forwards affair. A too-full life carries us by tides, currents and seasons that take us with them – whether we wish it or not. We may deceive ourselves that we are in charge of our destinies, but no; we're at the beck and call of the crammed filofax, the ever-ringing mobile phone, the stream of e-mails. We're part of the dance routine of twenty-first century back-packers. In the words of that cliché of utter banality that could have been uttered by the Teacher himself, we've *been there, done that, got the teeshirt*. And none of it amounts to anything that can be taken into eternity, because the big thing – our life with God – has been blocked from view.

It is only after the litany, in chapter 3, of tearing down and building, scattering stones and gathering them, searching and giving up, that the gentlest of hints is given as the Teacher reveals his true colours in verse 11: *He has also set eternity in the hearts of men.*

Why is it that this vital dimension remains hidden to so many? It is because all the available files have been filled up, and none of them is marked *'God'*, or *'Building my Character'*, or even *'Establishing my relationship to the Universe'*.

Marilyn Monroe somehow personified the restless insecurity of the twentieth century. 'I've tried to change my ways,' she said, referring to her scatty lifestyle, 'but the things that make me late are too strong and too pleasing.'

Her life surely continues to speak to thoughtful people. Is it possible to be everywhere, yet nowhere? The answer seems to be 'Yes'. To be known and celebrated by millions of people, yet to be lost in terms of personal identity and lasting fulfilment? The Teacher of Ecclesiastes confirms

1. Os Guinness, *The Dust of Death,* Inter-Varsity Press, 1973, p. 223.

from his own experience – as someone who had everything – that it is all too possible.

To have identity eroded by the ceaseless cycle is to have *no direction!* To have energy wasted by the aimless life is to have *no centre!* To have eternity blocked by the full agenda is to have *no home!*

The road taken by Ecclesiastes is one of cold, hard logic. Have a look at your presuppositions! Follow them to their natural conclusion, and ask yourself how satisfied you are with your present world-view, and how well does it fit with your deepest instincts about life?

Os Guinness has written, 'There is always a tension between what people *say* they are, and *who* they are.'[1] He instances Issa, the Japanese poet of the eighteenth and nineteenth centuries. All five of his children died before he was thirty, and then his wife died as well. After one of these deaths he went to his master of Zen, and asked for an explanation of such suffering.

His tutor replied, 'Just as the sun rises and the dew evaporates, so on the wheel of suffering sorrow is transient; life is transient; *man* is transient.' That was Issa's religious answer, and, on returning home, he wrote a poem – which he found himself unable to finish. It began:

> *The world is dew...*
> *The world is dew...*
> *And yet...And yet...*

The poem was never finished. The 'and yet' explained the basic dilemma. For Issa, the orthodox Zen believer, life was nothing more than a drop of dew, soon to evaporate.

---

2. C.S. Lewis, *Surprised by Joy,* Collins, 1955, p. 189.

But for Issa the father and husband, crushed by bereavement, agonised by grief, the sheer logic of his feelings and emotions told him that life must be more significant than *that!*

Just to think along these lines is enough to alter one's whole view of life. *He has set eternity in the hearts of men.* 'Is it possible, then, that I have been conned into believing a binful of lies? Is it not time for my intellect to catch up with my deepest human instincts about love and life; the creation, and the future, and God?'

It need not take much! For the intellectual C.S. Lewis, the actual change of world-view was a matter of minutes only:

I know very well when, but hardly how, the final step was taken. I was driven to Whipsnade one sunny morning. When we set out I did not believe that Jesus Christ is the Son of God, and when we reached the zoo I did. Yet I had not exactly spent the journey in thought. Nor in great emotion. 'Emotional' is perhaps the last word we can apply to some of the most important events. It was more like when a man, after long sleep, still lying motionless in bed, becomes aware that he is now awake.[2]

6

'If you can meet with
Triumph and Disaster
And treat those two
Imposters just the same'

('If' – Rudyard Kipling, 1910)

Ten minutes quiet may be enough. Away from the clangour, the lights, the distractions of high living that so cluttered the life of tragic Marilyn Monroe, Ecclesiastes can be our tutor, prodding us with our own logic, insistently and patiently: *Yes, in your spirit you are just about dead. But you can change now, to a new world of thought and belief, where love, and forgiveness, and sacrifice and prayer begin to operate. Trust the lesson of the Teacher. All along you are being prompted to know God and his Son Jesus Christ, who loves you and has died for you. It is not too late. You are not on the River of No Return.*

Randolph Lycett of Australia was persevering valiantly on Wimbledon's Centre Court. It was 1921 and he was playing Zenzo Shimidsu of Japan in the quarter finals. The match was played on one of the hottest days in memory, and Lycett felt obliged to revive himself with gin every time the players changed ends.

John Olliff of *The Daily Telegraph* later reported: 'The fifth set provided perhaps the most extraordinary spectacle ever seen at Wimbledon. It was a long set of twenty games, and in the middle of it, it became apparent that Lycett was on his last legs. He could not go on drinking any more gin, because the combination of the gin and the heat of the sun was making him feel extremely muzzy. On the other hand, he was in desperate need of some further stimulant. He then did the most courageous and unprecedented thing in the history of Wimbledon. He ordered a bottle of champagne to be brought out on to the Centre Court for him.

'It was placed on the umpire's chair for him, and he consumed the last drop of it as the umpire called the score,

---

1. John Olliff, *The Romance of Wimbledon,* Hutchinson, 1949, p. 53.

"Shimidsu leads by nine games to eight in the final set". By now Lycett was beginning to stagger about the court. At one time the spectators were sympathising with him, at another they were angry, and at another moment they were laughing. They did not know which to do when he fell and dropped his racket, and then, on hands and knees, crawled round in search of it. To every one's relief Shimidsu won 6-3, 9-11, 3-6, 6-2, 10-8, and so Lycett was forgiven for his indiscretion.'

What days they were! Lycett lived to fight again another day, and reached the final the following year. Those were the days of the true amateur, when people played tennis solely for the love of the sport. It was at that time that the words of the quotation heading this chapter were engraved over the portals of Wimbledon's Centre Court:

> *If you can meet with Triumph and Disaster*
> *And treat those two Imposters just the same*

Rudyard Kipling's famous poem was entitled simply *If* – but it could just as fittingly have been called *The Art of Frustration*, for it is a eulogy to the enduring spirit that persists, like Randolph Lycett, in the face of every trial and disaster. The last round, the final straight, the fifth set! Translate that into every arena of living, whether political, domestic or commercial – and you are into the philosophy – no, the *theology* – of Perseverance, in an imperfect and fallen world.

It is to do with the tension of finding yourself poised between Triumph and Disaster; stranded between A and B; having begun, but not yet having finished. It is the tension of living – and waiting – during the 'In-Between' times, those boring, dull periods of life when you are longing for the breakthrough which refuses to come. Our civilization is full of exponents of the principle. Let us select the Christian apostle, Paul of Tarsus, as our example. Here he is, writing to that infant church in Philippi, the first foothold of the gospel in all Europe:

> I have learned to be content whatever the circumstances. I know what it is to be in need, and I know what it is to have plenty. I have learned the secret of being content in any and every situation, whether well fed or hungry, whether living in plenty or in want. I can do everything through him who gives me strength (Phil. 4:11-13).

Content (v.11) is a key word. In the Greek it is *autarkeia*. It is an entirely non-religious, 'secular' word. In ancient literature it was used by the Stoics of old – with whom Paul was familiar. The Stoics were a school of Greek philosophers founded by a man called Zeno, 308 years before Jesus was born. Their central plank of belief was that virtue was the highest good, and that all passions and desires should be rigidly subdued to the great priorities of discipline, endurance, control and fortitude. We sometimes use the phrase, 'Stoic courage', to describe someone of outstanding durability.

The ideas of the Stoics had persisted to the time of the New Testament and the apostle Paul. 'Autarkeia' means *sufficiency, self-sufficiency, competence, self-mastery*. The Greek lexicon describes 'autarkeia' as 'the state of one who supports himself without aid from others'. And that, of course, was a favourite characteristic hailed by the Stoics.

However, once we come to the New Testament, the apostle Paul seems to inject the word with an entirely new quality of meaning. It takes on a 'God' dimension that wasn't there before. When writing to his readers at Corinth, he makes his financial appeal on behalf of the poor at Jerusalem, and then promises, 'And *God* is able to make all grace abound to you, so that in all things at all times, having *all that you need* (autarkeian), you will abound in every good work' (2 Cor. 9:8). Again, when writing to Timothy his colleague, Paul states, 'But *godliness* with *contentment* (autarkeias) is great gain' (1 Tim. 6:6).

It only remains for Philippians 4:11, instanced above, to complete the trio of references to 'autarkeia' in the New Testament – and we can see what the apostle has done. The word has altered its meaning, almost imperceptibly, but significantly. No longer is it made to mean *self*-mastery. In each of the three uses, the context indicates a *God*-centredness that has been built in. It is only because of Christ that Paul can say of his own experience that he has learned to be *content*.

So it is 'autarkeia' – this God-centred capacity to *manage,* to *endure,* to be *content* with every circumstance – that puts substance and meaning into daily living. 'Autarkeia' is what imparts significance to people of every walk of life, whether they are computer programmers, students, cab drivers or telephone operators. Or indeed Christian ministers such as Paul.

I have learned to be content whatever the circumstances.

These words were not given from an armchair or lecture podium but from a prison cell – by a man who on his very first venture into Europe finds himself, in Philippi, accused unjustly, beaten and put in the stocks. Now here he is, writing to those same people in Philippi, and once again in prison!

Kipling, then, is right on target. These lines from his poem illustrate the principles in view:

> If you can keep your head when all about you
> Are losing theirs and blaming it on you,
> If you can wait and not be tired by waiting,
> If you can bear to hear the truth you've spoken
> Twisted by knaves to make a trap for fools,
> And so hold on when there is nothing in you
> Except the Will which says to them 'Hold on!'
> Yours is the Earth and everything that's in it,
> And – which is more – you'll be a Man, my son!

It happens to people every day; the creative producer in the studio whose best productions are hacked to bits by an editor and end up in small pieces on the cutting room floor...the athlete hampered by an unforeseen injury...the church minister whose fresh ideas for the running of the church are tossed out of the window by an unfeeling council. Ultimately, it is the truly goal-orientated operators – with the long-term view – who can learn to step back and view their reverses against the backdrop of the wider scene.

Back to tennis. Take Boris Becker, victim of an upset win at Wimbledon years ago. 'What went wrong?' he was asked in the television interview afterwards. The blue eyes opened wide in surprise: '*Wrong?* Nothing has gone wrong. Nobody has died! I lost at tennis, right?'

Tennis again: Here is John Bromwich of Sydney, Australia. Inbetween tennis practice he does his milk round; he's a real amateur. Much loved by the crowds. But now it's July 1948, and he's reached the final of Wimbledon against Bob Falkenberg of USA – and he's standing at match point! Up goes a weak shot from Falkenberg who is way out of court; all John has to do is gently *pat* the ball over the net. Instead he excitedly slams it – and it goes out. Falkenberg goes on to win. The crowd is in tears. End of Bromwich? Well, hardly – he always has his milk round to go back to! *That was his job.* And the crowds never stopped loving this particular Aussie.

Take Borotra. Yes, tennis again! Borotra was the French champion of the twenties. He got so popular he had to get his faithful chauffeur Albert to sign his autographs for him. The present-day Centre Court at Wimbledon was built to accommodate the extra crowds who turned out to see the Bounding Basque. An amateur always, however, he was philosophical about both winning and losing; he was actually a businessman in his daily life. My only meeting with him was when he was ninety; he turned up at the memorial service for commentator Dan Maskell – held in our church of All Souls.

'It's an honour to meet you at last,' I exclaimed over a cup of tea afterwards. 'You *made* Wimbledon'.

'Ah, non!' he smiled back. 'Wimbledon – it made *me*!' He paused, gallantly, to kiss the hand of a lady admirer.

This is the point. When your triumph is snatched away, when your energies are fading and your props are removed, *who are you?* Look again at Paul – how would you summarise this giant of the church? A brilliant evangelist? The greatest debater of the age? Lecturer in three languages? The informed traveller of the Mediterranean basin? The most influential theologian of the last two thousand years? The enemies of the Christian faith could see the threat represented by this man.

Very well, *bang him into jail.* Neutralise his abilities! Take away his books. Chain him to a guard and shut him up tight! Paul is nothing now.

And so it might have been but for Paul's sense of completeness in Christ alone, and the flexibility of outlook that could learn to convert a prison cell into a broadcasting studio. True, they've got the preacher captive – but Paul now has his own captive audience, courtesy of the Roman Caesar! The letter from prison slips out to inform his friends:

> Now I want you to know, brothers, that what has happened to me has really served to advance the gospel. As a result, it has become clear throughout the whole palace guard and to everyone else that I am in chains for Christ. Because of my chains, most of the brothers in the Lord have been encouraged to speak the word of God more courageously and fearlessly (Phil. 1:12-14).

Perhaps it was with a smile of irony that Paul was able to add this salutation to the end of his letter: 'All the saints send you greetings, *especially those who belong to Caesar's household.*' It was the gentlest of hints that the imperial arrest of a Christian was the surest way of starting a church at the very seat of power!

Once believers in Christ become integrated with the Christian framework of thinking that was Paul's, we have a starting point far ahead of the rest. We should be able, through this 'contentment' within the will of Christ, to handle the most complex and trying of circumstances , like a juggler with fifteen balls in the air.

A great bundle of tensions confronts the beginner, and one of the secrets of progress is to see adversity as part of normal Christian living, and to learn to live with it. This is basic to the New Testament, wrote Hugh Silvester:

In practice when suffering comes, the Christian (if he is anything like me) says, 'Why me? Why should this happen? Am I not a child of God?' He regards suffering as an interruption, an unwelcome interlude. When it is over he can get on once more with living a 'fruitful' Christian life. Not so; suffering *is* the Christian life. 'Since therefore Christ suffered in the flesh, arm yourselves with the same thought.'[2]

If we can understand that difficulties are a necessary part of Christian discipleship, we shall never have to face the perpetual disillusionment confronting people of other world-views, for example, the traditional Marxists of old. The Marxists always believed in a kind of Utopian ideal, attainable here on this earth. *They were always going to be disappointed.* It is inevitable that such ideologies will eventually cave in and leave their supporters stranded.

We in the church have never thought in terms of a perfectible society *in this life.* We are certainly called to aim high: indeed, to aim for perfection – the very top! In moral terms, we are called by God to be 'perfect', as he is. Did we expect anything else – that our Leader, the purest being that has ever walked on earth, would ask us, please, to try and sin a little *less?* No, to settle for anything short of 100 per cent makes us already 'backsliders'! We are, then, to make the standard of Christ himself our aim, nothing less – but knowing meanwhile that it is not going to be achieved this side of the grave. *We can live with this tension, once we understand it.*

We can also learn to live with the same adversities and hostilities of the unredeemed world that confronted Paul and his companions – and even make them work to the

---

2. Hugh Silvester, *Arguing with God,* InterVarsity Press, 1966, p. 117.

advantage of God and his kingdom. This is 'the art of frustration' – to come to terms with these things and turn them to advantage. It is a learned art – when frustrations can be transformed into an internal dynamo of creativity and service!

We knew a missionary called Ken Ogden. He used his skills as a carpenter and builder to good effect in one of the developing countries. At one point he had shown his local pupils how to build a church. They did it together. They were just about to embark on the final lesson of making the seating, when the blow fell. The totalitarian government of the day found fault with Ken and ordered him out of the country at twenty-four hours notice.

What would you have done? Run round to the bank, and try to extricate what funds you could? Scraped up your most precious belongings, and frantically gathered all together for a hasty exit? Ken did none of that. Those last hours he spent with his pupils, and made *one seat* for the new church. 'There!' he said, when it was done. 'There's your model. Now I'm going, but you finish the rest.' He left them, not only with the prototype for a church seat, but also with a standard of how an integrated Christian behaves under pressure. It was the lesson of *autarkeia*.

'*I have learned the secret*,' wrote Paul. When did he learn it, and how? Was it an instantaneous thing, when the vision and call of Christ was given on the Damascus Road? Certainly it began there. What kept Paul in those times of shipwreck, mob violence and imprisonment? When man after man let him down and left him without support? Why, it was the fact that he was an apostle; he knew that he had been sent! In the last analysis it is *only* those with a sense of call who are still in the field when everything has gone wrong.

But in another way the lesson is only learnt over a lifetime, through hardship, pain and disappointment. The twentieth century, as in no century since the first three, highlighted the resilience of Christian faith where the church was tested by fire – in war zones, tyrannies and killing fields. A Rwandan bishop – after many brushes with death in the mid-1990s – described how, in one locality, many of his people had been killed. Some, who had managed to escape the massacre, had gathered with him. It was Sunday, at around midday.

'From the top of the hill,' he said, 'we could see hundreds of people coming, armed with various weapons. They stopped at a distance from us. We had been praying for two days and teaching people how to receive Jesus Christ, to repent of their sins and to prepare for heaven. Three people came and told me, "Bishop, we come to tell you that people are coming to kill you."

'The words that came into my mind were from 2 Kings, when Elisha, the servant of God, was surrounded by an army of angels, bigger than that of the enemies who were coming to destroy him. I told these people, "You go and tell them that this hill is surrounded by many angels. If these angels allow you, then you will come and destroy us. But if they don't allow you, nobody will approach us. So we are ready. Go and tell them that we are ready. We are not afraid."

'We waited. Thirty minutes later, they just stopped a hundred metres short of the hill where we were. Then we saw them going away, and I was aware that it was the angels who had restrained the army which was surrounding this hill' *(Church Mission Society News*, April 1995*)*.

Triumph or Disaster? They had been ready for either. And then, which is the harder – the immediate crisis or the slow ordeal? The death squad or the grinding prison sentence? Steve Biko or Nelson Mandela? Again, the apostle Paul was ready for either. Perhaps the hardest was waiting in prison and not knowing. Waiting is always hard!

The greater part of our lives is taken up with *waiting* for the next thing to happen. Waiting for news of the expected baby...for the examination results to come through... for the long-distance flight arrival at JFK... for the next vacation... for promotion... for the reports of the medical test... for the elusive answer to prayer – it's hard to wait! *But it is what we do with the waiting times of life that determines the kind of people we are going to become.*

If you can wait, and not be tired by waiting...

We incline to think that it is the high, soaring moments of achievement that are significant, but it is not so. It is all too possible to spend a decade wishing your life away! It's what you do with those boring, frustrating, 'in-between' periods that makes the difference between effectiveness and superficiality. We have to believe, as Paul did, that God himself is at work when apparently nothing is happening! 'My Father is always at his work to this very day,' said Jesus, 'and I, too, am working' (John 5:17). God is just as alive, just as personally involved and active five minutes *before* the awaited breakthrough – when the answer to prayer still seems a million miles away – as he is five minutes *after.*

Autarkeia. All this is tightly tied into theology. The Christian is essentially, deep down, an *in-between person.* We work and witness as people living between the first appearance of Jesus Christ – in his earthly ministry – and his return at the end of the age. It is a period full of tensions for the Christian church. There is advance across all five continents, and the final Triumph is assured, but along the way there will be frustrations, setbacks, persecutions, martyrdoms – and the non-stop attrition of the world, the flesh and the Devil!

Learn this lesson of biblical, godly sufficiency, and keep in the learners' lane – developing a framework that will hold when everything around us seems to fall apart. That way we shall fulfil the goal of the whole of our lives, which is to grow in Christ-likeness. We are in the fellowship of the In-Betweens! At times it feels like Triumph *now*. Often it looks like Disaster. The trick is to do a Kipling and treat *both* as perhaps Randolph Lycett did, in his Centre Court epic with Shimidsu. But this time without the gin.

7

'That's one small step for
a man, one giant leap
for mankind'

(Astronaut, Neil Armstrong,
21 July 1969)

Bishop Trevor Huddleston, famed for his human rights record during South Africa's apartheid days, was telling of his experiences at the time of the moon landing in July 1969 – and I was in the room.

'I was standing in the typical African bush of Tanzania that very day,' he recalled, 'and I was listening intently to a little radio I had with me, as Neil Armstrong's voice crackled dramatically through space: *One small step for a man, one giant leap for mankind.*

'Just by my side was a small inquisitive African boy. "Who is that speaking?" he asked, "what is he saying, and where is he speaking *from*?"

'For the life of me,' continued Huddleston, 'I could not find the language to explain the drama of what was taking place just then. I simply gave him what I later realised was the most brilliant reply I could ever have given. "Ni muntu," I explained briefly. *It is a man.*'

In those four words lies the explanation behind the age-long voyage of discovery embarked upon by the human race – from the first flint axe right through to the space rocket; through the agrarian, industrial and microprocessor revolutions up to the present day.

It is a man.

Naturally it is to the Bible that we must turn for the only satisfying answer to the question of our own identity as a race. *Who* are we – *what* are we – that we should be capable of such exploits? Just to look at the advances that have taken place in the twentieth century! Assuming the average human lifetime to last for some sixty-two years, Alvin Toffler highlighted the point some years ago:

Only in the last seventy lifetimes, has it been possible to communicate effectively from one lifetime to another, as writing made possible to do. Only during the last six lifetimes did masses of people ever see a printed word. Only during the last four has it been possible to measure time with any precision. Only in the last two has anyone anywhere used an electric motor. And the overwhelming majority of all the material goods that we use in daily life today have been developed within the present lifetime.[1]

We can expect the pace to quicken further. But this will not be because modern innovators are any cleverer than, say, Aristarchus of Samos, who around 270 BC, anticipated Copernicus by eighteen hundred years in his conviction that the earth was not flat, but a sphere travelling around the sun. In our basic human make-up, we have not essentially changed. Anthropologists have traditionally used such categories as *homo erectus* and *homo sapiens* in their study of our past. But I believe that it was John Stott who first coined the term *Homo Divinus* in his basic definition of a human being; someone who is characterised by the original stamp of the image of God, and therefore capable of worship, prayer and fellowship with the Creator. The surrounding creation is our environment, and it is our home!

> Then God said, 'Let us make man in our image, in our likeness, and let them rule over the fish of the sea and the birds of the air, over the livestock, over all the earth, and over all the creatures that move along the ground.'

1. Alvin Toffler, *Future Shock,* Bantam, 1970, p. 14.

> So God created man in his own image, in the image of God he created him; male and female he created them.
>
> God blessed them and said to them, 'Be fruitful and increase in number; fill the earth and subdue it' (Gen. 1: 26-28).

Is this easy to believe, situated, as we are, on a planet that is only an astronomical atom among our surrounding, whirling constellations? In our sun alone, there is room for one and a quarter million earths such as ours. And the sun itself is only one star among a great group of such stars. On beyond the Milky Way, in immeasurable distances, are yet other systems such as that of Andromeda, with its countless suns.

And yet the stars are very thinly scattered in the universe. To bring the scale down a bit, supposing a star were just the size of a pinhead, and were placed here on earth – it would be between twenty and thirty miles from its nearest neighbour. Is it easy to believe that all this was purpose-designed as our home?

Stephen Hawking of Cambridge University describes the earth in these terms:

> ...a medium-sized planet, orbiting round an average star in the outer suburbs of an ordinary spiral galaxy, which is itself only one of about a million million galaxies in the observable universe. Yet the strong anthropic principle would claim that this whole, vast construction exists simply for our sake. This is very hard to believe.[2]

---

2. Stephen Hawking, *A Brief History of Time*, Bantam Press, 1988, p.120

It is more than hard to believe; it is impossible – without an authoritative *witness* that can stand astride and outside all of our history and scientific probings, a witness that can stand the test of time. We have this in the biblical record. For it is the Bible that gives us our proper perspective, and corrects the flaw in Stephen Hawking's world-view, for all his brilliance. What is noteworthy is what was *left out* of Hawking's statement.

First, there is the factor of *God*-centredness, not man-centredness, in our fantastic universe. Secondly, Hawking fails to take into account the possibility that creation could be the home, not just of the human *species* as such, but of a race of God-like beings! That is our stature and calling. And thirdly, we must never forget that the whole of creation centres in... *a Man,* who is described in the Scriptures as the image of the invisible God, the heir of all creation, in whom everything holds together, and for whom it all consists. He is Jesus Christ, fully God and fully human. He is the prototype human being, and it is only in relationship to him, the Lord of all creation, that our residence in the immensity of this cosmic home begins to lose its absurdity. Here then is an account of our origin and home – that can satisfy a tribe in a developing country, or a business person in a hotel room, reading the Gideon Bible.

Ni Muntu.... it is a Man! James Irwin, one of the American moon astronauts, worshipped and spoke at our London church on one occasion. He gave us a framed photograph of the moon landing. Under the picture he had added a caption in his own hand. It reads, *God walking on the earth is more important than man walking on the moon.*

Irwin's point was important. It may be that journeys can be made to the moon, to Mars even, or Neptune. But what is the whole thing *for?* The revelation – and it has to be a revelation from God for us to grasp it at all – is that there is a Creator, and that he is concerned personally about this world and its inhabitants. This realisation unlocks so many philosophical puzzles.

In opposition to atheism, the Bible proclaims *God*. In opposition to polytheism and the belief in many gods, the Scriptures emphasise *one* God. In opposition to Pantheism, which identifies God with nature, the Bible declares the *separateness* of God from his creation. In opposition to materialism, we learn of the *spirituality* of God and of the human race. In opposition to Deism – the concept of a world wound up like a watch and then left alone by an absentee God – the Bible declares that God the Creator is also God the *sustainer,* and furthermore that he is God the *intervener* in our affairs and our history.

It is God in Christ, then, and not just an amazing world as such, that provides the true background and proper identity to *Homo Divinus*. Before the two opening chapters of Genesis are over, the reader is beginning to get some answers. As a Chinese man once exclaimed, 'Whoever made this book made *me*!'

This is the message of the grand overture to all the Scriptures – that behind all that we can see, know, sense and are, is the God of all creativity, the originator of the universe. Of course we are not here faced with an account as a journalist would have presented it. No person was present to see the creation of the world in any case. It is the emphasis that is so important.

Science places much emphasis on the stages following the original Big Bang – the formation of the continents, oceans, vegetation and the animal kingdom – as taking place over many millions of years. So vast are the statistics that our own apparently short history is reduced in significance to virtually vanishing point. But the Bible reverses that proportion and turns it completely around:

'The forming of the continents? Those tortuous procedures, those millions of years that are said to have gone into the creation of the first jellies and crustaceans, and the forming of the mosses, the trees – and the dinosaurs? *A week's work, that's all.* We'll give that bit a page. *Correction* – we'll give it two pages! And then the real bit, *your* story; the bit that those experts of yours dismiss as a single page? Why, we'll need well over a thousand pages before we're through!'

In the face of the countless galaxies and the billions of years that shrink us, we would feel completely lost but for this divine word that puts the balance right and gives us orientation and *size*. And responsibility!

> Let them rule over the fish of the sea and the birds of the air...over all the creatures...(Gen.1:26).

Rule...not exploit! The human responsibility is to be one of care and custodianship over the world of nature. Our concern is to extend beyond the earth itself, and into the heavens and the cosmos as well – hence the areas of astronomy and space exploration. We have only to refer to the New Testament letter to the Romans for this wider involvement to be apparent:

> The creation waits in eager expectation for the sons of God to be revealed. For the creation was subjected to frustration, not by its own choice, but by the will of the one who subjected it, in hope that the creation itself will be liberated from its bondage to decay and brought into the glorious freedom of the children of God (Rom. 8:19-21).

It is evident that the destiny of the human race is strangely locked into that of all the created order; both are waiting for the future 'liberation' – for the redemption of our bodies (Rom. 8:23), but also for the new heaven and the new earth that Scripture promises. So space exploration? If carried out responsibly, yes. It is part of our domain.

We are cast in the role of God's estate managers. We are separated from the animal kingdom and are placed over it and all the created order – not by dint of brute force, but as trustees who are to govern, husband and protect the earth's resources, to name and categorise the animals; thus there is the beginning of zoology and science.

We are in the image of God; that tells us of our high calling – but also of our limitation. We are *images* of God, but only images. We are not God himself; we exist only by derivation, unlike Christ who is the exact replica of God (Col. 1:15). For this reason the New Age teaching will one day fall flat on its face. You can, after all, persuade tired business executives in New Age seminars that they have a god inside them and that there is nothing that they cannot achieve. But it will not be long before it becomes all too obvious that they have been sold a lie; they are failing to meet their deadlines, failing to satisfy their spouses, suffering from duodenal ulcers and ingrowing toenails – manifestly they are *not* God!

Only one thing was stated *not* to be good, in those first two chapters of Genesis, and that was that the man was alone. So Genesis chapter 2 gives us the Magna Carta of sexuality and marriage, and the summons to community. We were made for each other, side by side, male and female – with the *differences* between the sexes being, as one writer has put it, 'the single most important fact of human society'.

After all, it would be unthinkable to say, 'In Oxford Street, *a human being* asked me the way to Trafalgar Square!'

Again, who are we? The Bible's definition of Genesis 1:27 places us on a far higher level than the secular humanist, or indeed a few clerics on the extreme edge of the church's life. The Rev. Don Cupitt, who frequently graced British television screens in the 1980s, no longer believed in an objective God. But it also appeared that he scarcely believed in himself:

> My self is a mere temporary aggregation of processes...My own desires are part of the flux of forces in nature.[3]

I only wonder what suitable format could be found for the communication of such sentiments. The pastoral interview? The pulpit? The Sunday School? The deathbed?

No, we are *Homo Divinus* – raised to our status by the God of creativity, of personality and of responsibility. Chapter 2 of Genesis places the man in his garden, somewhere near where the rivers Tigris and Euphrates flow close together. Perhaps our human race had its beginnings a few miles west of Baghdad? The point is that already in the Bible story, place names are being featured; it is not just a fairy tale. Here are the beginnings, not only of science and zoology, but the taking seriously of geography too.

The truth is, we were not intended to forage for ourselves out in the jungle or the desert; we were to be in the place, the garden, the *home* appointed by God. Our responsibility was to keep the garden, to look after it and to observe its laws.

---

3. Scott Cowdell, *Atheist Priest?*, SCM Press, 1991, p. 62.

And the tree of the knowledge of good and evil? The implication is that Adam would not have known what good and evil were, unless he transgressed. The choice facing him, then, was not between good and evil, but between God and himself. We may ask: 'Should we have been made with this capacity to choose against God? But if fellowship with God is to mean anything at all, there has to exist the possibility of refusal. Otherwise we are no more than robots, reduced to the level of machine programming.

The Fall takes place, and it is real. Did it take place in heaven – with Satan – *before* it happened on earth – with the guilty pair? The right answer is that it is conceived as *one* fall, not two. It is advisable to avoid applying standards of modern chronology to God's account of the Fall.

Although the image of God upon us is defaced by the Fall, it is not obliterated. Again and again we are able to see flashes of the heights that men and women can attain, irrespective of whether they are religious. In times of crisis, or faced by the challenges of nature, we have it in us to rise to the occasion, as noble King man, as regal Queen woman!

An example took place some years ago when an airliner crashed into the Potomac River. Scenes from the disaster were flashed on TV screens everywhere. One of the most vivid incidents recorded was of a man on the bank throwing off his jacket and plunging into the river to rescue a young woman victim of the crash, who was drowning. His name was Lenny Skutnik. Ignoring the rescue services, the helicopters and the television crews, he reached the girl, got her to the bank, and then melted quietly away into the crowd. Only later did his identity become known. In that moment of rescue we saw King man as he ought to be, the apex of God's creation.

Was such an event entirely predictable? Was Lenny Skutnik *not* responsible for his actions; was it all attributable to his genetic make-up? The glib theorists can sound plausible enough in a lecture room or TV studio. They become totally irrelevant in the great moments of human crisis, surging emotion or supreme creativity. We are people, not machines. It is within our capacity, even as sinful rebels, to love, to sacrifice and dedicate, because of who we are.

It is the Michelangelos of this world, the Nelson Mandelas, the Florence Nightingales and Joni Earecksons who explode the theory that we are no more than blobs of protoplasm wrapped around an appetite. Our ultimate model, however, is not to be found among these inspirers. Nor are we turning to Plato, Aristotle or Isaac Newton.

One model alone is enough. He is permanent and he is universal. We should let this description of Christ burn into our mindset:

> He who descended is the very one who ascended higher than all the heavens, *in order to fill the whole universe* (Eph. 4:10).

The whole universe centres around a human being! Of course there are those who carry out earnest research into the possible existence of other forms of life in the universe, little green men and all – but we could save them the bother if they only knew. God is a human being, and we who are made in his likeness, though we have fallen from our original stature, are called back by the gospel of the Cross and Resurrection, to aspire to know him, the prototype human, Jesus Christ. Only as we commit ourselves to him will all of our existence begin to make sense and take on significance. For what is to be found at the centre of the universe?

It is a Man. And not only so, but *with* him there at the centre, is his redeemed church! The *church* at the centre of the universe? I can hear the emperor Domitian laughing in the first century AD – 'The *church?* What's that?' Later on it's Stalin – 'The *church?* How many armoured divisions have they?'

But we go along with the apostle Paul. He takes as already established this indissoluble link between Jesus and his friends. Christ's destiny is our destiny!

> The first man was of the dust of the earth, the second man from heaven. As was the earthly man, so are those who are of the earth; and as is the man from heaven, so also are those who are of heaven. And just as we have borne the likeness of the earthly man, so shall we bear the likeness of the man from heaven (1 Cor. 15:47-49).

It is one small step that is required, not at the foot of a lunar module, but at the foot of a Roman cross. *It is the only place where God will meet us.* Here lies the difference between staying as an earthly human being, unforgiven and without a future hope, and making the giant leap to a place at the side of the man from heaven, Christ, Master of the universe. To come to know him, follow him and become progressively like him is literally the space adventure of a lifetime.

8

'The moment the slave
resolves that he will no
longer be a slave, his
fetters fall'

(Mahatma Gandhi, 1949)

Liz and I stood above the valley, gazing down in awe at the Pont du Gard, the sensational Roman aqueduct near Nimes in Southern France. Built by slave labour before the time of Christ, there it stood, column upon mighty column in perfect preservation. It is so massive that its base is used as a busy motor thoroughfare to this day. We found ourselves compelled to return a few days later for a second visit.

The fact that so many of the celebrated monuments of the world are associated with slavery and oppression should send a pang through the thoughtful visitor. The pyramids of Egypt are a prime example. The Taj Mahal in India is said to be the most beautiful building in the world; but its beauty is marred by the ugly truth that when its hundreds of workers had completed their task, they all had their eyes put out, so that they would never build anything as beautiful again. In Rome it is entirely appropriate that the Coliseum is now officially designated a memorial to the Christian martyrs who met their deaths there.

When we look back a century or two, Mohandas Karamchand Gandhi is widely hailed as one of the great champions of the oppressed. Born in 1869, he was renowned for his prolonged fight against racial legislation in South Africa, and then in India for his civil disobedience campaigns in the struggle for home rule. *Mahatma* ('Great Soul') Gandhi became venerated across India for his self-discipline, for his commitment to non-violence and his championing of the underclass; not least the 'Untouchables' of the caste system – whom he renamed *Harijans* ('Children of God'). How could people know freedom from slavery – politically, socially or internally within themselves? This was a theme running through his life:

The moment the slave resolves that he will no longer be a slave, his fetters fall. He frees himself, and shows the way to others. Freedom and slavery are mental states.[1]

Gandhi's sentiments can be paralleled with those of a black American slave, Frederick Douglass, a century earlier. Writing in 1845, he described how, the moment his master's mistress had introduced him to reading and writing, the seed of self-conscious thought was sown in his life. From that point on, it was impossible mentally to go back:

> I have observed this in my experience of slavery, that whenever my condition was improved, instead of its increasing my contentment, it only increased my desire to be free, and set me to thinking of plans to gain my freedom. I have found that, to make a contented slave, it is necessary to make a thoughtless one.[2]

This has always been true. Hence the determination of all authoritarian regimes, without exception, to keep the education of their slave class at the lowest possible level. Anything to stave off that dangerous moment of self-consciousness, when an entire people, even, may come alive and defy the ruling powers, and start to live as they were born to live. But how is that moment arrived at? Here undoubtedly lay an area of frustration for Gandhi. *'He frees himself,'* is his phrase. Similarly with Douglass – *'My desire to be free.'*

---

1. *Non-Violence in Peace and War*, 1949, Vol. 2.
2. *Narrative of the life of Frederick Douglass, an American Slave,* The Norton Anthology of American Literature [5th edition], Vol. 1, W.W. Norton & Co., 1998, pp. 2044-5.

The vital question is: How? India became independent in 1947 ('the noblest act of the British nation'), but Gandhi's dream of a country united in peace and freedom was never fulfilled. So much that he campaigned against – poverty, cultural strife and the caste system – remained impenetrable to his influence. Half a million deaths from civil war, and the shock separation of Pakistan from India, were part of the darkening clouds surrounding the Mahatma before his death at the hands of a Hindu fanatic on 30 January 1948.

Gandhi's single-minded contribution to India's independence firmly established him as one of the great leaders of the twentieth century. But India was never able to shake herself loose from the inner turmoils inherited from her cultural past. *How then is it done* – freeing an entire people from the 'fetters', of whatever kind, that hold it down? The issue has confronted protagonists for freedom and national unity from Moses onwards.

A classic example centres on the prophet Ezekiel in the middle of the sixth century BC. He had been caught up in the tragedy that had overwhelmed Israel and Judah, in three successive deportations of the Jewish people by the Babylonian king, Nebuchadnezzar. Ezekiel had found himself, together with thousands of his fellow citizens, forcibly exiled to an area about fifty miles south of modern Baghdad. It was slave labour there, in a heat of over 100^0F. Five hundred miles away, the holy city of Jerusalem was now a scene of complete destruction. It was the worst thing that had ever happened to God's chosen people.

It was when they were ten years into their ordeal that Ezekiel, the Jews' remarkable seer, received one of those luminous prophetic visions that characterised his long career – the Valley of the Dry Bones! Here was an opportunity for a people with a slave mentality to become 'thoughtful', and to gain at least an inner spiritual freedom. Here was a revelation that would inspire Ezekiel and generations of leaders after him, faced by people stuck in a captive, no change situation. The vision holds a key of priceless value for every civilisation:

> The hand of the LORD was upon me, and he brought me out by the Spirit of the LORD and set me in the middle of a valley; it was full of bones. He led me to and fro among them, and I saw a great many bones on the floor of the valley, bones that were very dry. He asked me, 'Son of man, can these bones live?' (Ezek. 37:1-3).

Ezekiel stood above the valley, gazing down in awe at the scene below. Was the vision coloured, perhaps, by Ezekiel's own memory of thousands of corpses, resulting from Nebuchadnezzar's conquest? The picture is stark and grim. This is where slavery to Babylon has brought you! Dry bones; irreversible catastrophe. Israel will never rise again. *Stop thinking*.

A hopeless case

If the captives had entertained any hopes of a reprieve when they had first arrived in Babylonia, those hopes would by now have been sunk without trace in the marshy swamps that surrounded the Euphrates. The mentality had become dull, memories of past glories had dried up; spiritual hardening of the arteries had set in, and devotion, prayer and worship had become arid, dead things.

It can happen to a nation, it can happen to a church, it can happen to spiritual leaders and it can happen to you. It is possible to become *accustomed* to a narrow, earthbound existence, and even to find a certain security in such captivity. When this takes place in a community, language becomes gross and coarse, awe disappears, the sky becomes closed off, and worship is a bore. No amount of public exhortations will wake up a people when death has set in. You can make resolutions, advertise on hoardings, write in the radical press and free up the rules of admission! Nothing will change.

Here, in Ezekiel's people, was a nation that had been singled by God out of all history, to bring his light and rule to the world! But something in the corporate spirit had died. It looked like a no-hope diagnosis: 'Son of man, these bones are the whole house of Israel' (v.11). And the crunch question comes, *Son of man, can these bones live?*

The logical answer would seem to be 'No'. There is little chance of a slave 'resolving that he will no longer be a slave', once the mentality has been stifled, the spirit killed, and opportunity crushed in ruins five hundred miles away. As it is, Ezekiel gives a diplomatic answer: 'O Sovereign LORD, you alone know.' It is then that the prophet is given his task:

> Then he said to me, 'Prophesy to these bones and say to them, "Dry bones, hear the word of the LORD! This is what the Sovereign LORD says to these bones: I will make breath enter you, and you will come to life. I will attach tendons to you and make flesh come upon you and cover you with skin; I will put breath in you, and you will come to life. Then you will know that I am the LORD"' (Ezek. 37:4-6).

Have you ever heard of the Wesleyan revival? Of the awakenings in America under Jonathan Edwards and Charles Finney? Of the Welsh, the East African, the Korean revivals of faith? It is passages such as Ezekiel 37 that repeatedly inspire belief that the blood and fire of the Christian Gospel are as powerful today as in the first century of the Christian mission. But never did a mission field or congregation look such a hopeless case as Ezekiel's!

A useless task

The dead, dry bones of Ezekiel's vision are completely stripped, and scattered over the valley. Yes, death is complete. However, the power of the word of God is such that even a universe can be preached into being! It follows then that lifeless, dead bones – bleached and dried in the relentless sun of Babylonia – can be prophesied into life again. And so the prophet is given his mandate. It looks absurd:

Preach to the bones!

'Er... yes, right. To the bones? Over there? Um... it won't do any good, Lord. You see, we haven't had any temple worship for the last decade. It's hopeless... and after all, the Christian group at my campus has died on its feet, Lord... It's no good trying to reach my particular group of colleagues; they're as hard as nails... Don't ask me to try and win *my* family for Jesus Christ – might as well try and communicate to a bunch of dried-up Egyptian mummies! ...*You see, Lord, we're now living in a post-temple era.*'

'Never mind all that,' comes the command. 'Preach to them anyway.'

And then, as Ezekiel complies, a stirring begins; there's a rattling and a shaking in response to the words of the prophet. It's a miracle. He sees the hip bone connecting to the thigh bone, and the thigh bone connecting to the knee bone – as they hear the word of the Lord!

In his vision, Ezekiel watches it happen – but all through history *we* have watched it happen too.

Come, for example, to the crunch day for Europe –
24 August AD410. The end has come for Rome and for all
Christendom. Yes, it all happens on a single day. There are
simply too many Barbarians around for civilised society to
contain any longer. Alaric, leader of the Visigoth hordes, is
at the very gates of a city that for so long has stood for the
stability and unity of all Europe. Then the unbelievable
happens. Rome is sacked, *Rome!* Word gets around. It's all
over. Despite the emperor Constantine's earlier conversion
and subsequent establishing of Christianity as the State
religion in AD324, everything solid has come apart. Rome
is sacked... dead bones everywhere. Christianity has failed.
If only we'd stuck with the pagan gods all along!

Over in Carthage, a middle-aged man of fifty-six chose to
disagree with this diagnosis, as the shocking news reached him.
He was Augustine, Bishop of Hippo. Rome – was it worth
preserving anyway? Surely, he reasoned with his Christian
friends, every earthly city falls eventually. Christianity had
never been interested in preserving *Rome!* We have always
been citizens of another and eternal City.

Augustine began to write, as he rallied the Christian
believers of shattered Europe. *It is not all over.* He compared
Rome's destruction with that of Sodom, and encouraged
his friends to focus instead on the Bible's vision of the City
of God:

> There will be an end to every earthly kingdom. You
> are surprised that the world is losing its grip and full
> of passing tribulations. Do not hold onto the old man,
> the world; do not refuse to regain your youth in
> Christ, who says to you: 'The world is passing away,
> the world is short of breath. Do not fear, thy youth
> shall be renewed as an eagle.'[3]

3. Augustine, *De Civitate Dei*, AD412-427.

The City of God was a monumental work of twenty-two volumes. It took Augustine fifteen years to write. Its impact was colossal. It helped to remake a single community for all of Europe, centred at base level upon the objective truth of Scripture. Without Jesus Christ, Europe would not have been – *and never will be* – anything more than a collection of competing Barbarian tribes! The combination of Augustine and his contemporary, Jerome – whose life work was the Vulgate version of the Bible – produced for Europe a single, great culture which was to endure for the next thousand years.

The scattered bones can be reconstituted a unity, and given flesh and breath! *It has been done before; it can be done again.*

Could not Gandhi have done something of this kind for India? The answer, reluctantly, is 'No'. Gandhi, for all of his fascination with Jesus (his favourite hymn was *When I survey the wondrous Cross*), never could come to the conviction of a single, all-encompassing and integrating Truth, that followers of Christ ascribe to him alone. Gandhi was a Hindu, and in his view every tradition had its own differing and complementary 'truth'. He was unable to cope with the idea that *one* great teaching could possibly be true in itself. His world-view was comprised of 'all that I know to be best in Islam, Christianity, Buddhism and Zoroastrianism'.

There can never be unity along that road. Gandhi's solution for India of uniting Muslims and Hindus met with total failure.

How can one unite a society and rid it of the elements that keep it in mental slavery? Ezekiel was to share the great secret with the world, in his vision of the valley of the dry bones. It is done by the Word of God and the Spirit of God. Nothing else will bring integration to a community.

'**Prophesy to these bones** and say to them 'Dry bones, hear the word of the LORD... Then he said to me, '**Prophesy to the breath**... and say to it, 'This is what the Sovereign LORD says: Come from the four winds, O breath, and breathe into these slain, that they may live' (Ezek. 37:4, 9).

There were then — and are — two necessary parts to the operation; the communication of God's *Word*, and the animation of God's breath, or *Spirit*. This is reminiscent of the book of Genesis, where God *speaks* — and the initial act of our creation takes place — and *breathes* — and man becomes a living being.

Preach to the bones... and address yourself to the Spirit. It is as the twin activities of preaching and prayer are engaged that the miracle takes place in Ezekiel's valley. As though a divine wand has been waved over them, the entire, disintegrated confusion of dead skeletons becomes a living, vibrant army of animated people. A hopeless case? A useless task? History would say 'No'!

An impossible dream

It certainly looks impossible — restoration from the death of slavery in a foreign land to a rejuvenated army with a message for the whole world!

Therefore prophesy and say to them: 'This is what the Sovereign LORD says: O my people, I am going to open your graves and bring you up from them; I will bring you back to the land of Israel... I will put my Spirit in you and you will live, and I will settle you in your own land' (Ezek. 37:12-14).

This indeed took place. As in the case of Rome's overthrow, Babylon fell on a single day, 16 October 539BC, under the leadership of Darius, co-regent of Cyrus of the Medes and Persians. Cyrus himself entered the city seventeen days later, amid scenes of jubilation, and shortly afterwards proclaimed the decree that let the slaves return to their own land. It has been said that Judah went into exile as a nation, and returned to her land as a church.

But the fulfilment of Bible prophecy always goes beyond the immediate circumstances of the original utterance. We have to see a secondary fulfilment of Ezekiel's vision in the New Testament people of the gospel, set free from the bonds of sin and death by the preaching of Jesus and his death upon the Cross. Then there is a still further fulfilment of the prophecy – in the far-off reaches of the End Times – with the rejuvenation of our tired, dying world in the new heaven and the new earth that all history is pointing us towards. If you believe that, then you have a cohesive world-view which is going to affect everything that you touch!

It is not an impossible dream. The bones can and will live! At times doubts will raise themselves. In the middle ages, Europe seemed to have lost its way spiritually, with salvation obscured under a welter of error and superstitious practices. But then, as Erasmus observed in a letter of 1519, *The world is waking out of a long, deep sleep.* The great Reformation of Luther and Calvin followed – which Erasmus had helped to usher in by his massive scholarship – and once again the yoke of spiritual slavery under a corrupt system was lifted on a vast scale. Four hundred years later my own life and that of millions of others are profoundly affected by that Reformation – an open Bible, a clear view of salvation and an unshackled spirit. Later still after the

Reformation came a further release of the human spirit in the Wesleyan revival:

> My chains fell off, my heart was free,
> I rose, went forth and followed thee!

No amount of sociological campaigning, or inter-faith manoeuvring, can bring about such a radical liberation. It is here that we sense the wistfulness of Mahatma Gandhi, and the extraordinary lengths to which he went in his spiritual search:

> What I want to achieve – what I have been striving and pining to achieve these thirty years – is self-realization, to see God face to face, to attain *Moksha* (spiritual deliverance)... I have not yet found Him, but I am seeking after Him... For it is an unbroken fortune to me that I am still so far from Him... I have not seen Him, neither have I known Him.[4]

It is Jesus who gave the vital clue to all human searching, when he declared to doubting Thomas, 'If you really knew me, you would know my Father as well. From now on, *you do know him and have seen him*' (John 14:7).

This possibility is open to all who recognise in Christ the way, the truth and the life; that universally and exclusively, he is the only way to the Father (John 14: 6). A child can come this way. And so can a slave of the Roman empire.

The Christian slaves of the first century are a model for us all! A great proportion of the Gentile church was initially composed of such slaves – the very people who built the

---

4. *An Autobiography,* J. Cape, 1949, p. 252.

Pont du Gard aqueduct. But what was their status as Christian slaves? How should they now behave? Present a petition to Caesar? Organise a sit-in, a protest march, a people's revolution? Attempt to throw off their Roman fetters in a violent uprising? But that would have been to reduce their leader Jesus Christ to the level of a mere Spartacus or Che Guevara.

In the event, they were inspired to do something more revolutionary still. Within the Christian fellowship they began to treat the social classifications *as though they didn't exist at all.* Christians, such as the Roman slaveowner Philemon, found themselves challenged by a new code, as in the test case of a returned runaway slave, one Onesimus. The apostle Paul's letter to Philemon was like a time bomb, awaiting its future moment of detonation through Christian reformers such as Wilberforce and Shaftesbury. For the time being, the recommended action over Onesimus the slave was very simple:

> Perhaps the reason he was separated from you for a little while was that you might have him back for good – no longer as a slave, but better than a slave, as a dear brother. He is very dear to me but even dearer to you, both as a man and as a brother in the Lord (Philemon 15, 16).

The days of official legislation against slavery in civilised countries still lay far ahead. What do you do in the meantime? The apostle Paul was clear in his advice to Philemon: *Just do it in your own household – live like a Christian!*

That, after all, is the best laboratory for a testcase. Not the law courts so much as your own living room – 'the church that meets in your home,' writes Paul (Philemon 2). The Christian meeting at Philemon's place was about to experience a small revolution. As the fellowship and prayer time ended, no longer would Onesimus the slave then be allowed to enter the room, carrying the pizzas, only to depart again. He was now to be one of the circle, taking his part in the mutual support and the sharing of prayer requests. Paul is very clear:

> You are all sons of God through faith in Christ Jesus ...There is neither Jew nor Greek, slave nor free, male nor female, for you are all one in Christ Jesus (Gal. 3:26-28).

In that first century the slaves were just about the only available working models of this principle. If you were looking for an attractive lifestyle to emulate, Paul would have pointed you to the slaves of Crete, whom he expected to 'make the teaching about God our Saviour *attractive*' (Titus 2:10). If a slave can do it, then anyone can do it!

And that is how social revolutions are achieved; simply by enough people living as Christians – taught by the Word of God, and inspired by the Spirit of God. It is actually happening in practice all over the world, and in some of the hardest arenas ever known – in Southern Sudan, in central Asia, in Indonesia and China.

Wherever we are we must practise this ourselves. Even if you are only one in six billion, there is always something that calls out to be done. Pornography on the Internet may worry us – but we are to see to it that pornography has no entry point within our own homes. We may fret over the decline in the institution of marriage; then the standards of Christ must rule in our own private lives. We may lament the tight-fistedness of governments in dealing with world debt – but are we tight-fisted ourselves?

The world may well stagger in confusion and disillusionment in these opening years of the third millennium. It certainly did after the AD1,000 mark was passed. The Word and the Spirit of Ezekiel's vision provide the lesson for us: the Bible and Prayer. *How dull that sounds!* But do it anyway, and you will find to your amazement that you are part of the fulfilment of Ezekiel's vision – a living member of *a vast army*. And dull it won't be.

9

'I'd like to be a Queen in people's hearts'

(Diana, Princess of Wales, 20 November 1995)

It was early in the morning when the telephone shrilled beside me. I was sitting at my desk in our London home, thinking about the Sunday that lay ahead of us at All Souls Church. I picked up the receiver. It was my Australian colleague, Richard Trist.

'Richard?' he started.

'O, hullo, Richard. How are you doing?'

'Fine, thanks. But I was wondering whether we ought to do anything different to the morning services in view of the news.'

'News? I haven't heard anything.' I began to feel shaky.

'It's Princess Di. I'm afraid she's been killed.'

There are only a very few of the great public crises in which everyone can remember precisely where they were and what they were doing when the news story broke for them. I was on the doorstep of my parents' home in Tonbridge, on the evening of Thursday, 23 November 1963, when the door opened and my mother came out, distraught. 'Have you heard about Kennedy?'

'No. Mum. What's happened?'

'He's been assassinated.'

Now it was Diana. I staggered for some minutes. Then it came to me; there wasn't a moment to lose. *Church this morning.* Steadily, Richard Trist and I went over the checklist. Our preaching colleague Rico Tice must alter his sermon. Our director of music, Noël Tredinnick, must change the music; in the event he omitted the first hymn and played a lament instead. Church Council member Alison Grieve would have to be rung about the prayers – had she heard the news yet? Then I must give out a careful announcement, for the benefit of those who would arrive at church not having heard of the stunning events.

Everything would be coloured by what had happened in the Alma tunnel in the early hours of that fateful Sunday. Days later I was asked to write a page for the *Sunday Express*. Before long I was to be interviewed on an American TV programme – simply because we were in London and had ready access to the crowds, the atmosphere in the underground trains and on the streets. And, of course, in the church.

There's nothing like a very public death to shake the world, to make millions catch their breath and think long and hard about the 'Candle in the Wind' that represents every person's short, flickering life. **'I'd like to be a Queen in people's hearts, but I don't see myself being Queen of this country,'** Princess Di had told BBC interviewer Martin Bashir fifteen months earlier. Now she was gone – and the remembered remark was reflected in the many 'heart' emblems that featured in thousands of messages and flowers that descended upon Buckingham Palace and Kensington Palace. The most celebrated woman on earth had died in a Paris underpass, and the reverberations went worldwide. Indeed for weeks afterwards, I took extra care over my driving. If I was in an underpass, my thoughts would immediately switch to the events in the Alma tunnel. Crossing the road, I would be more alert than usual. Everyone had been made more aware of their own frailty.

But all the shakings of history, warns the Bible, are only curtain-raisers to the universal shaking that will take place at the end of the world – when the only thing to survive Christ's return and the great day of judgment will be what the Scripture describes as *the kingdom that cannot be shaken:*

See to it that you do not refuse him who speaks. If they did not escape when they refused him who warned them on earth, how much less will we, if we turn away from him who warns us from heaven? At that time his voice shook the earth, but now he has promised, 'Once more I will shake not only the earth but also the heavens'...

Therefore, since we are receiving a kingdom that cannot be shaken, let us be thankful, and so worship God acceptably with reverence and awe, for 'our God is a consuming fire' (Heb. 12:25-26, 28-29).

The biblical writer is saying that the earth has had its times of shaking. Far ahead of the time of Christ, those people of Israel felt *their* world shaking around them – as God's giving to them of the Ten Commandments forged them into a nation... as the divine Covenantal contract was hammered out in smoke and rumblings at the sacred mountain of Sinai... as the Jebusites, Amorites and Perizzites tumbled one after another into the dust around them... in the adventure of the great trek towards the Promised Land.

The battles! The crises! The judgments! And, in our own time, the unexpected twists and turns of a climactic twentieth century that have shaken our media-driven world, as none other. But – warn the Scriptures – these are only the prelude to the final crisis! They are given to point men and women to the only entity that will survive *everything* – the 'kingdom that cannot be shaken', whose members are declared to be *the first-born, whose names are written in heaven* (Heb. 12:23).

There is something personally significant about getting your name onto a roll or register, or – as millions did in September 1997 – into one of the books of condolence that were opened for Princess Diana all over the world. The act gives permanent recognition to something that you have done or decided; you are now established in the annals. *It has become official.* A similar phenomenon featured on the streets of London, where a million people lined the route for the funeral procession of Queen Elizabeth the Queen Mother in April 2002. A million of us felt we had to be there, and somehow *register*.

However, our writer to the Hebrews declares that only one register matters eternally, when the final convulsions of history end with Christ's return and the supremacy of the unshakeable kingdom. To have your name 'written in heaven' stamps you into the annals of eternity; you are in what Revelation chapter 20 calls *the book of life*.

This connects with the death of Diana, Princess of Wales. For the tragedy of the Alma tunnel aroused a number of very deep-seated instincts in people. Of course we must firmly set aside the hype – even religious hype, of the 'prophecy' brand that immediately jumped in and predicted a nationwide revival of faith within weeks. Plenty of mad legends were flying around; the Internet was thick with conspiracy theories. I refer rather to what the Daily Mail columnist Paul Johnson pleaded for. **'Give us a spiritual dimension. For Diana's sake, tell us that life has a purpose, and give us an idea of what that purpose is.'**

There were, perhaps, four great human instincts that lay behind the worldwide outpouring of grief and the reverent crowds that lined London's streets. Four widespread yearnings – and coupled with them we may recognise how the message of God in Jesus Christ *meets* people at the precise point of these felt desires:

The desire to atone

How could matters be put *right* with someone who was now irrevocably removed from all chance of reparation to her for damage inflicted? Diana was perceived at her death as a woman of beauty, fragility and compassion, who had apparently died in the process of escaping from the very predatory cameras that were feeding the public's appetite.

Michael Ignatieff, writing in *Prospect* magazine, commented, 'Sorrow is more intense when compounded of guilt, and ours was a guilty sorrow. We all had a hand in making the myths which killed her.'

Part of the guilt-ridding exercise was the hunt for a scapegoat. The *paparazzi?* The chauffeur? The Ritz Hotel? The House of Fayed? Who would take the chief burden of blame? And behind the bringing of flowers and the creating of little shrines by the Palace was the sentiment, *We are sorry; we seek for absolution.*

But there was another element present too:

The desire to unite

In a strange way people felt that they 'knew' Princess Diana. Somehow, in all her insecurities, she seemed close to ordinary people, deprived and buffeted people; consequently her death carried with it a remarkable *power* – as an American friend of ours put it – 'to give us something to make us *unified*'. In that sense there was something valid in her TV reference to being a queen in people's hearts. Many felt her empathy with the ordinary people.

Hence the enormous crowds – and I could sense, as I stood in the Mall to see the coffin going by, the reverence, the quiet, the feeling of mutual consideration and 'oneness' – of a kind reportedly not experienced in Britain since the testing days of World War II.

'It can't last, of course,' I murmured to a minister colleague, Paul Blackham, as we gazed at the quiet massed crowd outside Buckingham Palace. But it was a national phenomenon for about two weeks. Millions of people felt united by the power of a single person. There was great wistfulness. How could that mood be preserved...recreated? And how does God meet us – in the deeply-felt desires, to atone and to unite?

The desire to identify

It was impossible to ignore Princess Diana during her short life. Clive James, in the *New Yorker* (September 1997), noted the astonishing impact she made on virtually all nationalities:

> Diana once flew to Japan, addressed 125 million people *in their own language,* and made the most stunning impact there since Hirohito had declared that the war was over...
>
> She wasn't just beautiful. She was like the sun coming up; coming up giggling.

It was virtually impossible for anyone to stand outside this death. It had come after a whole series of signals that events were not under control, despite the final glimpse of fleeting happiness. So it was that millions of people felt a compulsion to identify, to *register* that they were not uncaring. Jean Seaton, writing in a magazine, commented, 'I (and many others) *worried* about Diana, like a wayward younger sister. When the dresses looked good, we felt pleased. When she looked frumpy, we felt irritated. When she took infant Will to Australia, us new mothers nodded with approval.'

Thus, when the news of the tragedy became known, there was something in people across the entire world that compelled them to go somewhere, do something, *sign and register*. There is, deep within the human spirit, a desire to place one's mark, to belong and to identify.

The desire to survive

That is, to survive in *ourselves*. Instinctively, many were thinking, *If even the celebrated Diana, surrounded by wealth, a protected VIP in a bullet-proof car – with a bodyguard – can have her life cut off in seconds at thirty-six years of age, what of me? And what is it all for, anyway? If I, too, could die just like that, where's the meaning? How can a person such as myself survive the shakings of life? How can I extend my own existence?*

I received this letter from a member of the public, unknown to me:

I remember me and my sisters were arguing during the funeral service whether Diana was in heaven... I am desperate to go to heaven when *I* am dead, although I am frightened of death too...

This instinct to survive is absolutely basic to human beings, across all the centuries.

In point of fact, all four of the desires that I have outlined above are essentially part of being human; they are with us all the time. It takes a crisis or an event of high public profile to strip us down a little, to the real person that we essentially are – God-like beings made for eternity – but under judgment for our sins, and restless with half-felt, unspoken desires to be *right*. They are the desires to **atone** for our faults and to know that we are free of guilt; to **unite** around something – or preferably *someone* – big enough to fill out the meaning of life in a lasting way; to **identify**, register and respond to something massive enough to demand our allegiance; and fourthly to **survive**, beyond the brittleness of this life, and to preserve the little candle flame... for ever!

On page after page of the Bible, we learn that God can meet us at every one of these four critical desires – supremely through his historical intervention in our world's affairs in the life, death, resurrection and triumph of Jesus Christ, who is none other than God in human form.

God in his book says, 'You want to atone for things said and done, and things not done too? To deal with all your guilt accumulated over many years – the guilt that you fear will one day find you caught out, unforgiven on the final day of reckoning when it's *your* turn?'

It is right to be concerned, for Hebrews chapter 12 reminds us that God is a consuming fire, and that there will be a judgment day, when everything unworthy will be shaken to pieces. But the same passage also tells us of Jesus, and of the 'sprinkled blood' of his death upon the Cross, through which God has intercepted his own judgment upon us. In this way our guilt – of whatever kind – can be atoned for, as an act of divine and free love. The condition of this forgiveness is given in verse 23 – '*You* **have come** *to God, the judge of all men, to the spirits of righteous men made perfect.*' But, we may ask: How can guilty people ever expect to be 'made perfect'?

It starts on the day we come to Jesus Christ, once crucified for us, for our forgiveness; and it is completed on the day when we die; when, as forgiven sinners, we are admitted to be with God – not as a flickering candle flame, but as God's living children who are to receive glorious resurrection *bodies*! The desire to atone for our sins is met by the atoning death of Jesus Christ. He has done it all.

And the desire to unite? To be unified around someone big enough to captivate the loyalties of great numbers of people from every culture and background? How I longed that the atmosphere of trust and togetherness experienced outside Buckingham Palace and Kensington Palace could have been maintained! The thought that Princess Diana might have been remembered as a Queen of people's hearts was a sentiment recalled and even embraced – but, as *Prospect* magazine commented only weeks after the funeral, *Already normality is returning.*

That was inevitable. But the unity theme can never be far away from the Christian church! I look around us in our own central London congregation, and I see – besides traditional Londoners – Australians, Koreans, Americans, Nigerians, Indians, Brazilians and scores of other nationalities.

There is only one factor that can possibly unite such a cosmopolitan crowd of people week after week, despite the many cultural differences. It is *Christ,* the man whose very public death in another historic city – that of Jerusalem – is *still* reverberating on, two thousand years later. It is he who unites us all, and not just on Sundays. In small groups we eat together, trust and support one another... and it is he who is the centre of the entire worldwide fellowship, putting the purpose and the meaning into our existence, within this widest and most all-embracing community of belief that there has ever been on earth. 'You have come,' enthuses our writer, 'to Mount Zion, to the heavenly Jerusalem, the city of the living God.' It is spoken of as already done, in and through a *person* who unites his followers permanently and eternally.

And the desire, thirdly, to identify? To register one's name when something tremendous is on? At the time of

Diana's death, many put their names in those books of condolence. Thousands of tributes to the Princess went into the Internet, designated to last in perpetuity. But in this world, nothing actually is for ever; least of all a web page on the Internet.

On the final day, when even the heavens are shaken and rolled up like a scroll, nothing will remain, except the things that 'cannot be shaken'. The only thing remaining will be the rule and kingdom of God. The desire to register, identify and belong is very strong within us. That instinct can only find lasting fulfilment when an individual moves on from a vague, perhaps nominal, interest in Christ and his church, registers his response to the Cross, signs up her commitment to the kingdom that cannot be shaken – and makes it personal. The name is then written in heaven; it goes into the book of life. *It has become official.*

And the fourth instinct – to survive as a person? The letter from my enquirer had asked, 'Is Diana in heaven?' Thankfully, it is not for us to pronounce as to who is and who is not specifically accepted by God, and particularly when we have no knowledge of a person at firsthand. That is God's business. We can certainly say that no one at all will quarrel with God's verdict, when the book is opened and the ultimate truth about people's hearts becomes known.

At the same time, a person may know *for themselves*, here and now in this life, that they are accepted by God! There is no need to wait until we die to discover our position. It is as I respond to all that Christ has done for me, in bearing my judgment at the Cross in my place, as I repent of my sins and accept him as my resurrected Lord; it is at that point that the assurance of his promised forgiveness, his friendship and free gift of eternal life, is chalked into the book on my account. And my name is there. *It's official.*

There is help for people on every side: books, churches – and programmes. A very effective programme I know is the internationally-known *Christianity Explored*, harnessed in its current form by Rico Tice, a colleague at All Souls Church. A meal, an introduction, then discussion and a chance to find out more.

And then, wherever we go, there will be Christian people about, who can help by their witness and friendship. I think of one such friend, a Christian layman Steve Rowe, who has given much of his spare time to openair preaching. Years ago in Kensington High Street, by a strange coincidence, Princess Diana was a few yards from him, by St Mary Abbotts Church. Steve felt bold enough to speak with her of his concern for her and the two princes, and asked her to receive a Christian pamphlet. It was entitled *Four Things God wants you to Know.* In no way was he rebuffed – quite the opposite. The princess accepted the pamphlet, and they parted amicably.

'Imagine my amazement,' Steve told me, 'when three months later she was in the same area. Again we had an opportunity for a brief word. "Do you remember, Ma'am," I said, "that I gave you a little leaflet some weeks ago?" Then she told me, "I've still got it." And yes, she had read it.'

Make it official for yourself. This very day. Use, if you will, this adaptation and expansion of the hymn, sung at both Diana's wedding and funeral – as an expression of your own prayerful decision to be part of the kingdom that cannot be shaken. It will still be there when everything else has gone.

I vow to you, my Saviour, all earthly things above,
Entire and whole and perfect, the service of my love;
The love that asks no questions, the love that stands the
test, That lays upon his altar the dearest and the best;
The love that never falters, the love that knows the price,
The love that stands indebted before your sacrifice.

And there's a royal country, I've heard of long ago,
It speaks of grace and heaven, a place that all may know;
We may not count her armies, we may not see her King;
Her emblem on a hilltop, the Cross of suffering,
And soul by soul and silently, her citizens increase,
Her ways are ways of gentleness and all her paths are
peace.

O tell me of the Kingdom, that stands the test of time,
O lead me to its gateway, and speak the word sublime
That tells me I'm forgiven, my name is in the Book,
The Cross of Jesus holds me, as heav'nward I look;
Baptised into a living hope, I'll walk the path that's new;
And the prize of God in Jesus, for ever I'll pursue.

So light the fire within me, and let me fan the flame,
And fill me with the Spirit, that I may bear your Name;
In season and in hardship, to run my given race,
O keep me ever burning, until I see your face;
I vow to you, my Saviour, that where your feet have trod,
I'll serve and follow faithfully, my Master and my God!

(After Sir Cecil Spring-Rice, 1859-1918, revised and
expanded, R.T. Bewes, *Jubilate Hymns*)

10

'I'm going to ask you to get up out of your seat'

(Billy Graham, twentieth-century evangelist to the world)

During the late 1880s, an evangelistic campaign was held by the renowned evangelist D.L. Moody in San Francisco. Just before it began, a professional photographer by the name of George B. Rieman offered to take Moody's photograph. He wanted to add the famous preacher to his collection of actors, politicians and other notables.

Moody declined the offer of a free sitting, saying that he had not come to San Francisco to have his photograph taken, but to save Rieman's soul. Rieman was beside himself with fury. But his curiosity had been aroused. On the very last day of the mission he attended the meeting, accompanied by his wife. After the sermon, an after-meeting was announced for enquirers. George Rieman turned to his wife: 'Well, we've been to the circus; let's go to the sideshow also.'

In the follow-up meeting, two Christian workers met with the couple, and by the end of the evening both had been led to faith in Christ. Rieman himself was to become an outstanding Christian preacher on the Pacific coast.[1]

What are the chances that two precious souls – besides a welcome new preacher – would have been lost to the kingdom of God, *if Moody had allowed his photograph to be taken?* But there was no risk of that. Moody was notorious for turning his back on photographers every time he saw them assembling their cumbersome equipment. He was altogether too focused on his calling as an evangelist to be seduced by diversions, adulation or titled personages. Or, for that matter, by money. His main weakness was exhibited in a fondness for pork and beans. It has been said of Moody that he put one hand on Britain and the other on America – and lifted the two countries closer to heaven. Many

1. John Pollock, *Moody without Sankey,* Christian Focus Publications, 1995, p. 230.

millions of people came to a first hand faith through this mighty preacher.

And what of his twentieth-century successor, Billy Graham? We are, perhaps, a little too close to him in time for a complete assessment of his ministry as yet. But without any doubt Billy Graham is the only evangelist there has ever been, of whom it could be said that he placed a hand on all five of our continents, in a ministry that has touched the entire world, and countless millions of people. By the time I, as a teenager, had heard him at London's Harringay Arena back in 1954, he had already spoken, face to face, to more people than any orator – secular or religious – in all of history. And that is leaving aside radio, television and films. My father, who was on his council, spoke to him just before Harringay began: 'What would you like to have come out of this?' 'Well,' said Billy gravely, 'among other things, at least a thousand missionaries.' Eventually he was to realise all of that, and much more – and in addition, the spawning of numerous Christian enterprises, begun by people who had been touched at Harringay.

The same phenomenon would follow at Madison Square Gardens, Melbourne cricket ground, the Maracana Stadium and a host of other centres. *African Enterprise*, of which I became UK Chairman some years ago, engages in evangelism and relief work in the great cities of Africa, and is truly African-led and African inspired. But it began in Madison Square Garden with a young white South African, Michael Cassidy, who was fired by the preaching of Billy Graham. Around the world it is virtually impossible to meet a gospel-centred family that has not, through one or other of its members, been influenced by this, the most effective of all the evangelists that the Christian church has ever had since New Testament days.

He kept it up, at Harringay Arena, night after night, for twelve weeks on end, as the campaign was repeatedly extended. Like Moody, Billy Graham was ruthlessly focused. Frequently a second meeting, and even a third, had to be hastily improvised in order to accommodate the crowds that kept coming. It was the only time in my life that I witnessed, repeatedly, the phenomenon of hymn-singing on the London underground, from one end of a train to the other – and all the way up the escalators. The most popular item by far was the theme song of the twelve weeks – *Blessed Assurance.*

It all culminated in an amazing final Saturday – when a capacity crowd, first of sixty thousand people, assembled at White City stadium, followed *the same day* by a second meeting at Wembley – the home of English football. For once, the stadium authorities made an exception to their regulations, and allowed the crowd to spill out onto the football pitch; and so a record attendance of 120,000 was set for Wembley, which in the nature of the case could never be equalled. As I sat high up in the stands that day, little did I fathom that the time would come many years later, when I would be Billy's chairman for another great London mission, and would hold the umbrella over him in a packed, rain-soaked rally – once again at Wembley! Later, in December 2001, Liz and I were to be enthralled witnesses of a ceremony in Washington DC, when the Queen honoured Dr Graham with the conferring on him of an honorary Knighthood.

His trademark phrase, repeated in football stadiums all over the world, has etched itself into the memory of the countless numbers who, in the course of over fifty years of preaching, made their way to the front of the platform in response to Christ's call. It remains among the most celebrated quotations of the twentieth century:

I'm going to ask you to get up out of your seat

Here was the summons by a world ambassador of the gospel, issued in ringing tones and with urgent sincerity. My own allotted task, when we first went as a family to the Harringay meetings, was to keep a watchful eye on my saintly grandmother. After all, her deceased clergyman husband Tommy had, as a boy of fourteen, 'gone forward' under the preaching of D.L. Moody, back in 1882. Now as Billy's invitation was given, Evelyn Bewes' great desire was to demonstrate her ardent support and go forward with hundreds of others. My job was to hold her in check. We reasoned that once she got down there at the front we'd never see her again! I could feel her fidgeting beside me, as the choir began to sing *Just as I am.*

'No, Granny,' I would firmly whisper, 'this is for *others.* We have to *pray* for these people as they make their decision... no – *Granny*!'

It was among the most formative three months of my life. Night after night I would attend. Sometimes we would have guests with us. And all the time something was drumming inside me, **You** *are going to be doing this too – for the rest of your life.*

There is no higher calling than to be an ambassador of Christ's good news... and the wonder is, every believer is appointed to this office, regardless of whether we are public preachers or not. It is what the apostle Paul describes as 'the ministry of reconciliation'. It is something we share with all Christians, worldwide:

Since, then, we know what it is to fear the Lord, we try to persuade men.... For Christ's love compels us, because we are convinced that one died for all, and therefore all died. And he died for all, that those who live should no longer live for themselves but for him who died for them and was raised again... Therefore, if anyone is in Christ, he is a new creation; the old has gone, the new has come! All this is from God, who reconciled us to himself through Christ and gave us the ministry of reconciliation... We are therefore Christ's ambassadors, as though God were making his appeal through us. We implore you on Christ's behalf: Be reconciled to God. God made him who had no sin to be sin for us, so that in him we might become the righteousness of God...(2 Cor. 5:11, 14, 15, 17, 18-21).

Fear...persuade...reconcile...ambassadors...appeal...implore. The passage is shot through with the pleading pathos and apostolic authenticity that has characterised such inspirers of the world as Richard Baxter of the seventeenth century: *I preached, as never sure to preach again, and as a dying man to dying men.*

Baxter's outlook may be contrasted with that of a cynical theologian I met at Durham University, during a mission I was leading. It transpired that he was an atheist. 'So why theology for you?' I asked. *'It amuses me,'* came the reply. As well as I was able, I warned him of his dire situation. He is quite likely to end up as a wicked old man. Once involve yourself in the Scriptures of God; once come under exposure to the realities of the blood and the nails of the Cross, and so face the stark alternative between forgiveness and judgment; once hear the urgent summons to faith – whether thundered or whispered by a servant of God – *and a person cannot remain the same.* We either become opened up and softened by the gospel, or we become hardened to it. It's kill or cure; it's life or death, heaven or hell. Simply to be 'amused' is already to be under a cloud of judgment of one's own making.

Here, in this fifth chapter of 2 Corinthians, is a wonderful passage on the theme of what God has done in reconciling people to himself through the death of Christ – and how he involves his believing people in 'the ministry of reconciliation'. No one is too inexperienced for this, no one is too young, and no one is too old! An honoured missionary to Africa told us that on the day his retirement was due, the message that was waiting for him in his daily reading was, *Son, go work today in my vineyard*. We are to be in active service until we drop! There is a task out there, and it is urgent. **We are ambassadors for Christ.** There is a world of adventure in that description, and there is a lifetime of surprises beyond the many forbidding frontiers that we shall cross!

A cousin of mine, Robert De Berry, when ministering as a clergyman in Sheffield, England, felt impelled to pay a pastoral visit to a sex shop that was in his parish. Prepared by prayer and fully on guard, he entered the premises, equipped with nothing more impressive than his locally-produced parish magazine. He greeted the proprietor, had a few words with him and left the magazine on his counter. A few weeks later he repeated the visit. Little by little he built up an understanding with the sex shop proprietor, bringing nothing more than his parish magazine on each occasion. Eventually the proprietor came to a firm faith in Jesus Christ, wound up his business... and went to Africa as a missionary. *How are these things done?* Why, by the combination of certain elements that Christ looks for in each of his ambassadors:

An ambassador is compelled by both terror and love

Knowing therefore the terror of the Lord, we persuade men, writes Paul in verse 11 of our chapter (King James Version). The Greek word *phobos* (from which 'phobia' is derived) can mean anything from 'terror', through to 'fright', 'alarm', 'fear', 'reverence' and 'respect'. When it is used in the context of the actions of God in judgment, it invariably carries the stronger meaning, as it does here – for the previous sentence of the passage refers to 'the judgment seat of Christ'. Revelation 11:11 is a similar example.

It isn't simply, then, the terror of a servant of God entering a sex shop. It is that, of course – but it is more; in this instance it is the godly terror of responsibility before the Judge of all the earth. Earlier, Paul had written that the work of God's ministers 'will be shown for what it is, because the Day will bring it to light' (1 Cor. 3:13). We are sent as ambassadors of *Christ,* the universal Judge! In this awe-inspiring calling there should be a proper 'terror' of letting him down.

But Paul is also able to write that 'Christ's *love* compels us, because we are convinced that one died for all, and therefore all died' (v.14). The Cross, whose shadow falls right across the human race, is the greatest inspirer of love in action ever known.

In my father's battered photograph album is a faded sepia photograph that he took shortly after his arrival as a missionary in Africa in 1930, of an old, gaunt Englishman with an unkempt beard and nondescript clothes, but fixing the camera with a steely gaze. Underneath the picture was Dad's written caption, *C.T. Studd.* The photograph told it all. Charlie Studd, bred in luxury, and educated at Eton and Cambridge, had been the sporting idol of England in the early 1880s. Celebrated as a University and All-England cricketer, the great W.G. Grace had described Studd as 'the most brilliant member of a well-known cricketing family, and from 1881 to 1884 had few superiors as an all-round player... His style of batting was free and correct, and he scored largely and rapidly against the best bowlers of his time'.

The change began with D.L. Moody's visits to Britain, and the conversion of Studd's father. After his own profession of faith, Charlie took members of the England Test Team to hear Moody; and several told him later that they had accepted Christ. Before long, massive meetings for testimony and challenge were being held in Cambridge, Oxford, London, Bristol, Newcastle, Manchester, Leeds, Liverpool and Edinburgh... and the theme – a lost world for whom Christ died. It was love, inspired by the Cross, that lay behind this call for ambassadors of the gospel:

> If Jesus Christ be God, and died for me, then no
> sacrifice can be too great for me to make for Him.

So declared C.T. Studd. In his determination to serve Christ abroad, he was joined by six prominent university friends. The Boat Train pulled out of Victoria Station on 5 February 1885, taking *The Cambridge Seven*, as they were called, to Dover and Calais, Brindisi, Suez, Colombo and China. The rest is history. Studd died in the Congo, a year after the meeting with my father. A thousand African Christians saw him to his grave.[2]

Terror and love. They are both here in 2 Corinthians 5. They are necessary ingredients in the spirit of an ambassador prepared to go anywhere for Christ. But there is more:

2. J.C. Pollock, *The Cambridge Seven*, IVP, 1955, pp. 105-108.

An ambassador is invested with
both authority and humility

'We are therefore Christ's ambassadors,' writes Paul, '*as though God were making his appeal through us*' (v.20). It is a sensational statement. When the representative of God is at work, there are to be no apologies, no weak qualifications, no back-trackings. At the same time there should be an accompanying, self-effacing grace, for 'We are not trying to commend *ourselves*,' says Paul (v.12).

A good historical example is seen in the remarkable missionary and outreach work of Kate Booth, oldest daughter of the founder of the Salvation Army. *La Maréchale,* she was called, after her exploits in Paris. One of her very first public meetings in England was as a girl of sixteen, facing a rowdy 1,500-strong audience. 'When all else fails,' her father William had said, 'put on Katie!' She quelled the crowd with the opening words of her song: *The mountains and the hills will all flee away, and you will need a hiding place that day; O may we be ready.* Then into her text: 'Let me die the death of the righteous, and let my last end be as his.' Those who responded to her witness that day were only the first of many thousands who would discover Christ during her next seventy-five years as an ambassador of Christ.[3] She died just as Billy Graham's influence was beginning to touch Britain.

Authority and humility; boldness and grace. We are ambassadors, because we represent the sovereign Lord of the whole universe! But we are *only* ambassadors; we are not there for ourselves! Here now is a third combination of features that Jesus Christ looks for in his representatives:

---

3. Carolyn Scott, *The Heavenly Witch*, Hamish Hamilton, 1981, p. 19.

An ambassador is appointed both to plead and to warn

'We try to persuade men...the ministry of reconciliation...
We implore you on Christ's behalf: Be reconciled to God...'
  But Paul continues in his next chapter:

As God's fellow-workers we urge you not to receive
God's grace in vain. For he says, 'In the time of my
favour I heard you, and in the day of salvation I helped
you.' I tell you, now is the time of God's favour,
now is the day of salvation (2 Cor. 6:1, 2).

There is something in God's ambassador and evangelist that
longs for individuals to engage with the gospel, as the
moment of opportunity swings towards each person! When
I was about fifteen, the time arrived for the taking of the
school photograph. It only happened once in every five
years; it was your one opportunity to obtain a pictorial
record of your life, your time and your chums! There were
750 of us, arranged in a massive semi-circle, banked six high.
In the middle was the intrepid photographer, with a
motorised, swivelling camera.

'It's your one opportunity!' we were warned. 'As the
lens comes opposite you, respond and be at your best; it'll
never happen again – so no messing about!'

I still have the result; a photograph about a yard long;
my total school career pictorially compressed into a single
record. Occasionally I pull it out – so *that's* how the lens
caught me!

Come to the Gospel account in the New Testament.
Jesus is travelling through all of Galilee; he is God's lens of
love and concern, *focusing* upon the needs of men and
women, as he moves steadily from town to town. Those

who have any awareness at all recognise that this is the time of opportunity; the moment is now and the tide is *in!*

Jesus reaches Capernaum. Interest is high. Here are four friends, desperate to take the opportunity for their disabled friend – but how to get him through the crowds to Jesus? The venue is jammed full of people... there's nothing for it – through the roof! (Mark 2:1-12).

The focus swivels to a great crowd by the lake. Who will benefit from the opportunity? A woman! You can just see her as she manoeuvres her way through the mass of humanity, wriggling and squeezing... just to touch his clothes! Perhaps he will help her... *he does* (Mark 5:25-34).

Now it's Jericho's turn. It's the Messiah's last visit; he will never come again. There is Zacchaeus, the diminutive tax collector, high up in a tree to get an unobtrusive view, as the Light of the World goes by... but then, *panic* – the gaze of Jesus has focused on the taxman! With those eyes on him – and the commanding voice: *I'm going to ask you to come down out of that tree; to receive me into your home* – it was now or never! Zacchaeus humbly obeys, and finds salvation (Luke 19:1-10).

So, moving on from Jericho... but wait! A blind man is on the edge of the crowd. His cries stop Jesus in his tracks, on his way to achieve the salvation of the world. Everything stops as Bartimaeus grabs the opportunity, receives his sight – and then follows Jesus. It's goodbye to Jericho for ever.

Once to every generation comes the moment to decide! It is for the ambassador of the gospel to plead this message and to warn of the issues – in the sober knowledge that the favourable climate for the good news can switch as changeably as the weather. Shakespeare put it memorably:

There is a tide in the affairs of men, which, taken at the flood, leads on to fortune; omitted, all the voyage of their life is bound in shallows and in miseries. *(Julius Caesar)*

Charles John Ellicott writes in the same vein: 'There is, so to speak, a *now*, running through the ages. For each church and nation, for each individual soul, there is a golden present, which may never again recur, and in which lie boundless opportunities for the future.'

I'm going to ask you to get up out of your seat

In one of Billy Graham's visits to Britain, a coach driver, on depositing his passengers at the stadium, was invited to come into the meeting. He declined the opportunity. Night after night the offer was repeated, but he preferred to stay in his coach and read the paper. The campaign ended, and the opportunity was over. Then the driver lost his job, and struggled to find his way again. Months later he emigrated to Australia, and was successful in obtaining a new post – once again in his familiar role as coach driver. He turned up to work the first day.

'So where am I off to?'

'Ah yes,' came the reply. 'There's a coach trip for you to a sports stadium. It's a Billy Graham meeting!' This time, when the passengers invited their driver in for the meeting, there was no hesitation. He went in with them – and went forward at the end to make his response.

It's like a lens of love and compulsion. You cannot guarantee, when it turns on *you* – summoning you to come to Christ, to change your ways, to make the comeback – that the opportunity will return. Your moment is *now*. And hence the sense of responsibility and urgency required in anyone who is an ambassador of Jesus Christ!

Once to every generation comes the moment to decide;
In the clash of truth with falsehood, all must choose and all
must side.
On the rock of Christ's salvation stands or falls each
mortal soul;
And the choice goes by for ever, sealed in God's eternal
scroll!

Truth in every generation, fragile as a mountain flower,
Looks afresh for faithful guardians; who will speak in
danger's hour?
When the enemy advances, flooding in with lies out-
poured,
In the breach we'll fight together – raise a standard for
the Lord!

Saints in every generation kept the flame of truth alive;
In the face of death, defying thrones they knew would
not survive.
Heroes of the Cross of Jesus win with him in this our
day,
By his blood and by their witness – come and follow in
his way!

Christ in every generation; Greatest Name the world
has known;
Teachers, thinkers, faiths and cultures find their goal in
him alone.
His the truth and his the Kingdom, at his Cross our
paths divide;
Once to every generation comes the moment to
decide!

(R.T. Bewes, after J. Russell Lowell,
Jubilate Hymns and Hope Publishing Company)

11

'I did not have
sex with that woman'

(President Bill Clinton,
17 August 1998)

'Like to do a microphone test for us, Mr. President?'

It was 11 August 1984, and Ronald Reagan was about to engage in one of his regular meetings with the American press. Obligingly he spoke the following words into the microphones in front of him:

> My fellow Americans, I am pleased to tell you I just signed legislation which outlaws Russia forever. The bombing begins in five minutes.

It was only a microphone test, but the words – recorded by a media opportunist – went all over the world. I was in Germany the week after the gaffe, and the quote was splashed across the front of the weeklies. Relations between the USA and Russia were under severe strain!

Watch my lips...

President George Bush's three words ended up as one of the best-known quotations of the twentieth century. They landed him in terrible trouble.

It is an embarrassment to a great many American people that President Clinton's remark – in reply to widespread suggestions of a relationship with the White House staff trainee Monica Lewinsky – has become the most world-renowned and quoted sentence of any president to date:

> *I did not have sex with that woman*

It is a sadness also to friends of America, on this side of the Atlantic, where this book is being written. We take no delight in the scandal that broke over the president's head during the traumatic months of 1998, nor do we join in any of the ribaldry that surrounded it. Nor should we wish to dwell overlong on the details. But there may, perhaps, be some principles that thoughtful people can gain from Bill Clinton's moment of bombast.

Leadership has extra responsibility. This surely should be learnt from the beginning by all who are placed in any position of leadership – parents, teachers, clergy, lawyers and politicians. Even your most trivial remarks are going to be remembered long after you have forgotten that they were ever uttered!

I remember the inane comment of a British theologian. It related to a totally unfounded theory about the sexuality of our Lord. Six weeks later I was in Africa. His fatuous and idle musings had already reached the sixth form of a school in a dusty town of Tanzania. An obvious daily sentiment for any leader in the public eye ought to be, not 'Watch my lips', but *'Guard my lips'* (Psalm 141:3). Particularly when you are said to be the most powerful man around.

Truth has a price. Think of Pontius Pilate. 'I find no fault in this man', he had said, on examining the case made against Jesus. Yet, when it came to the crisis of decision, he found that he could not pay the price of what he knew was the truth. Yet the responsibility could not be avoided. Sunday by Sunday, the credal statement of millions of worshippers – *He was crucified under Pontius Pilate* – have established Pilate's as the second best-known name in all history.

If you want to stand by truth, you are likely to have to pay for it. But, once you decide that you cannot afford the price, you will lie, perjure yourself, abuse your power and bring disgrace upon those who have trusted you. Back in the 1930s, before he ever became United States President, Harry Truman wrote, 'A man not honourable in his marital relations is not usually honourable in any other.'[1]

1. David McCullough, *Truman*, Simon and Schuster, 1992, p. 186.

Nothing can be hidden. Especially has this been so in the goldfish bowl that is our world today – created by a ruthless media from the 1960s onwards. *It is all going to come out!* It is the height of naivety for a leader, in particular, to imagine that it could be anything different. Ultimately it is the judgment of Christ that is the underlying principle governing our every idle word and action:

> There is nothing concealed that will not be disclosed, or hidden that will not be made known. What you have said in the dark will be heard in the daylight, and what you have whispered in the ear in the inner rooms will be proclaimed from the roofs (Luke 12:2, 3).

The low value placed on truth, in today's secular culture, means that plenty of people stand to profit from every scandal – the bigger the better. Fat contracts can be signed for the rights to the story. The errant TV clergyman can tearfully repent – preferably in the full glare of the cameras. Soon he can be 'restored' to his ministry, and then write a bestseller. A nation will learn that a disgraced politician has *the full confidence* of the government leadership, despite his unearthed sins (usually called by the press 'peccadillos'). If anything, his exposure is likely to result in a surge of popularity.

This is the style in which the twentieth century ended. *But it is also the style in which the first century began.* The wheel has very nearly gone full circle; we are back to Athens and Rome all over again. Today we are facing what is virtually a 'new' pre-Christian era. Despite the sensational growth of the Christian church in many parts of the world, there are hundreds of millions of people who are unaware that there should be any accepted standard for behaviour.

Ethics are presented to them as totally fluctuating and relative in their value. The price tag on truth has been ripped away.

Sometimes it is clergy with an unbelieving attitude to Scripture who cause the damage. During the summer of 1999 I read two books on ethics, one by a layman – a professor of paediatrics at University College London – the other by one of our more extreme bishops. And who was the theologian of the two? It proved to be the layman, Professor John Wyatt. He came out so far ahead of the bishop as to permit no comparison. His book displayed a world-view based on Scripture that was able to take full account of the modern ethical issues that challenge us, and still come out at the end with an utterly cohesive and compelling value system.[2]

And the cleric? He made it to the front page of *The Times* with his 'controversial' argument that 'it is better to leave God out of the moral debate and find good human reasons for supporting the system or approach we advocate...We are now poised on the brink of having the freedom to shape the very genes that previously shaped us'. Basically, the argument dates back to the secular humanists of the 1960s who insisted that ethics were perfectly possible without religion. As a matter of fact the argument really dates back to the Garden of Eden, where the man and the woman agreed on *deciding for ourselves* – which is the title of the bishop's last chapter.[3] I used to wonder how the bishop could draw a salary for promoting a view which, if taken to its logical end, would find the most useful part of the Bible to be the maps at the very back.

---

2. John Wyatt, *Matters of Life and Death*, Inter-Varsity Press, 1998.
3. Richard Holloway, *Godless Morality*, Canongate, 1999, p. 151.

His arguments are not really new; they are old ghosts from the first century. Upon that century Christianity burst with a new morality that found its inspiration in Jesus, and met the old pagan order head on. The above-mentioned bishop can write of today's young people who can *'have sexual intercourse with each other whenever they feel like it, the way they have a cup of coffee or a hamburger'* .[4] It is no different from the accepted morality of the first century, described by William Barclay:

> Chastity was the one completely new virtue which Christianity brought into the world. In the ancient world, sexual relationships before and outside marriage were the normal and accepted practice. The sexual appetite was regarded as a thing to be gratified, not to be controlled.[5]

The Roman empire was bad enough at that time, but Greek morals were worse still. Demosthenes of old had written, 'We keep prostitutes for pleasure, we keep mistresses for the day-to-day needs of the body; we keep wives for the begetting of children and for the faithful guardianship of our homes.' Later on Seneca was to write, 'Women were married to be divorced, and divorced to be married.'

Was it ever easy? The human sex instinct was bound to present us with some tensions, simply *because* it is so wonderful and so powerful; for it is the second strongest instinct of all – the strongest being that for physical survival. Without the sex instinct, all human creativity, romance and our very continuance as a race would disappear.

---

4. Ibid, p. 60

5. William Barclay, *Daily Study Bible; Philippians,* St Andrews Press, 1959, p. 150.

The call for control on the part of the Christians was scoffed at by the second-century Roman philosopher Celsus. He flatly disbelieved that Christianity could achieve a change in lifestyle. 'There,' commented the historian T.R. Glover, 'lay the great surprise. The Christians came with a message of the highest conceivable morality... They expected a response; they preached repentance and reformation; and people did respond, they repented and lived new lives.'[6]

A new scale of values had come. It wasn't the standard of Homer or Plato. It was the standard of Jesus:

> For you know what instructions we gave you by the authority of the Lord Jesus.
>
> It is God's will that you should be sanctified: that you should avoid sexual immorality; that each of you should learn to control his own body in a way that is holy and honourable, not in passionate lust like the heathen, who do not know God... For God did not call us to be impure, but to live a holy life. Therefore, he who rejects this instruction does not reject man but God, who gives you his Holy Spirit (1 Thess. 4:2-5, 7, 8).

This is as applicable and valid for the twenty-first century as it was for the first. It is up to the followers of Christ, in the power and energy of the Spirit of God (v. 8), to offer an alternative and to set the pace!

An alternative framework

These Thessalonian believers of our passage were among the very first converts to the Christian faith in all Europe.

6. T.R. Glover, *The Influence of Christ in the Ancient World,* Cambridge University Press, 1933, p. 75.

In those early days of AD49 or 50, when the apostle Paul had first come among them (see Acts 17: 1-9), they would have found the prevailing moral standards around them to be an immediate challenge. They needed as much to *unlearn* as to learn! The long-held assumptions of contemporary morality were about to be challenged, then undermined and finally replaced. And what *are* the fallacies that across the ages need to be corrected by the superior incoming ethic of Jesus? Here are just four:

Chastity is not truncation. The popular view is that if someone has not experienced sexual intimacy, then they are only half a person; they don't really *know* life. Paul denies this in verse 5 of our passage – that we are not to indulge in the passion of lust like the heathen *who do not know God*. Who are the ignorant ones? It is those with a casual attitude to sex, he insists, who don't know their way around. 'You *know*,' he emphasises in verse 2, as he refers to Christ's alternative way.

The problem today is not that secular society is emphasising sex too much; it is not emphasising it *enough,* or completely. It is society that is suffering from the truncation of sex. When I went into an Oxford Street store to buy candles for my wife's birthday cake, I discovered that many novelties were on sale – including manufactured replicas of human sex organs, detached and neatly packaged for sale. *Now that is truncation*, sex dehumanised and reduced. Take God out of the picture and we are left, as Malcolm Muggeridge once put it, 'with a choice of megalomania or erotomania, the clenched fist or the phallus, Nietzsche or Sade, Hitler or D.H. Lawrence'. No, chastity is not truncation.

Innocence is not ignorance. It is widely assumed that not to have experimented in sexual activity is to be ignorant and at a disadvantage. But there are enough people around who are living denials of this view. I think, for example, of Lorna Bowden out on the mission field where I grew up in Kenya. *Auntie Lorna* was a single lady of uncertain age. Whether she had ever had a boyfriend simply wasn't the kind of question you could possibly have put to her. We knew her as a woman of modesty and of apparent innocence in matters of this kind – and she certainly wasn't the poorer for it. She was a complete person. Certainly she was modest!

She was the only missionary for many miles around who had ever given injections. When, therefore, requested by a large, male missionary by the name of Harvey Cantrell to administer an injection in his backside, Auntie Lorna went pink.

'Oh Harvey, that's rather difficult, isn't it? O dear, I feel a bit... Harvey whatever are we going to do?'

'Don't worry a bit, Lorna,' came the reply. 'You stand one side of the door; I'll stand the other – and you can do it through the keyhole!'

History doesn't relate what happened. Yes, she was modest and innocent – and interesting. She could make a flourless, sugarless, butterless, eggless cake, entirely out of bananas. She was creative and *alive* – and infinitely more interesting to us children than the boring, boozy *White Mischief* type of Kenya colonial settlers of that time. To us, *they* were the ignorant ones!

Wants are not needs. It's a fallacy to say that every individual has sexual 'needs', equivalent to the need for air, food and water. Richard Foster writes, 'No one has yet died from a lack of sexual intercourse. Many have lived full and satisfying lives without genital sex, including Jesus.'[7]

7. Richard Foster, *Money, Sex and Power,* Hodder & Stoughton, 1985, p. 152.

To understand this is helpful and liberating. The single person is not a half person. We should learn that the person who is living in a period of singleness, long or short, is the possessor of a charismatic gift. The apostle Paul describes the state of singleness as a *charisma* (1Cor. 7:7)

Permissiveness is not freedom. The strange thing is that as we have watched secularised society develop, it seems to have become a little 'greyer', more monotonous, less able to deliver. Young people are increasingly nervous as they witness the crashing failure that their elders are making of modern marriage:

> *My future career:* When I leave school I shall probably go to St. Paul's School, or the City of London, or King's College, Wimbledon. After that, I hope to go to the university. After that I will buy myself a house, a car, and furniture. I will probably get married, although at present I have doubts about it – because Mum spends half her time telling Dad off, for such things as buying the wrong beer, waking up the baby, and not keeping promises; and if this is the outcome of the weeding (sic), it isn't worth the salmon and a three storey cake (*Boy, 9 years of age, Twickenham, Middlesex*).

It is up to modern Christians of the third millennium to emulate their spiritual ancestors of two thousand years ago, and prove the superiority of their alternative framework for living.

An alternative authority

When the apostle Paul wrote to the Thessalonian church, he would have been only too aware of its stormy beginnings, for he – as visiting evangelist – had been thrown out of the city. The chief complaint about the apostolic messengers was that they were saying 'that there is another king, one called Jesus' (Acts 17:7).

Another king – and an alternative authority for life and conduct – was being proposed. Paul is careful in his letter to remind his readers that the radical lifestyle he is setting out for them had been given 'by the authority of the Lord Jesus' (1 Thess. 4:2). It is possible that he had in mind Christ's endorsement, in Matthew 19:4, of the great creation principle set out for all time at the beginning:

> For this reason a man will leave his father and mother and be united to his wife, and the two will become one flesh (Gen. 2:24).

Our Lord adds his comment: 'Therefore what God has joined together, let man not separate.' In quoting Genesis 2:24, Jesus was setting out again the proper context for the ordering of intimate relationships between people – a one-man/one-woman, monogamous, publicly recognised relationship for life. A precisely defined and altogether new and different situation is implied by the man 'leaving' his parents and being 'united' to his (one) wife. This principle cuts across the concept of a couple sleeping together as a private arrangement. The *basis* of the relationship is to be understood publicly. 'No,' says Genesis 2:24, 'let it be clearly understood what is happening; an actual change is taking place, that is to be publicly recognised. Someone is leaving the parent-child bond, and is entering upon a husband-wife relationship. *It is a transaction.*'

Some may maintain that in sleeping together as a private arrangement, a couple are only testing their compatibility. While, naturally, it is right to exercise great care before embarking upon a lifetime commitment, the argument is a false one. Leaving aside the biblical restriction of sex to the marriage relationship alone, it needs to be understood that full adjustment between two people can take many months, even years. To rely upon sleeping together as a test of compatibility could be disastrous – to the point that an experimenting couple could actually *lose* each other, when they need not. Again, in the event of an experimenting couple breaking up, does the *next* partnership start on the same basis? You can reach the point when someone is doing it for the third, the fourth time. And having got into the way of it before marriage, is the habit going to be dropped so easily *after* marriage?

Here is an alternative authority. The *God* words occur with frequency in our passage – pleasing God (v.1)... It is God's will (v.3)... heathen who do not know God (v.5) ... the Lord is an avenger (v.6)... for God did not call us to be impure (v.7)... He who rejects this instruction does not reject man but God (v.8). The bishop who advocates a *Godless Morality* would have to put a clear line right through this passage. For it presents an alternative framework, an alternative authority, to every attempt at a human-based ethic.

An alternative confidence

It is a remarkable fact of history that those first-century believers won their way over the private lifestyle that God in Christ calls his people to observe. All the sentences in 1 Thessalonians 4 emphasise the *difference* that is to be expected among them. And the Father, Son and Holy Spirit all feature in the passage. God, the glorious Trinity, is *for* us in the battle for purity! He has also given us, in the Christian fellowship, the 'love' of 'each other' (v.9).

It is a wonderful encouragement. We are not out there on our own, as we face a new millennium, with all its pressures and temptations. How to break an illicit partnership or deal with some fantasy or fad? Coping with habits that are basically a part of growing up? One of the great answers is to be with people! This is where the church comes into its own. It's *people* who can help to blunt the loneliness of an obsession. A small group of trusted people around us for Bible study and fellowship is a tremendous protection. It is for this reason that balance and care must be exercised when judging the faults of someone as highly placed as a President of the United States. Who surrounds the President? Upon whom can he rely? Who gives him fellowship, in this loneliest of positions?

The Christian fellowship provides an obvious setting, within which the sexual impulse can be harnassed and channelled in natural and positive ways; where respect and affection between the sexes can be safely expressed – without the blithe assumption that a brotherly or sisterly kiss or squeeze must inevitably end in bed. Teaming together, praying together, eating and serving together, and going out together in mixed groups – here is a framework for a rounded, personal lifestyle. And, additionally, a platform for future marriages that will be strong, stabilising *and Christian*.

The divorce rate in recent years is an indication of the urgency. In 1932, divorces in our own country numbered seven hundred during the course of a single year. By 1999 divorces were taking place at the rate of 480 *every day*. No marriage is without its dangers. Ruth Bell Graham once wrote in the light of her marriage to her evangelist husband, Billy:

People have warned with great effectiveness about the 'dangerous forties'. And even about the dangerous eighth year of marriage. (I can't recall that anything of moment occurred during the eighth year of our marriage in 1951.) But I am convinced that each year we are vulnerable...[8]

We do well to focus upon good models. The Grahams set an outstanding example, as did their predecessors in the nineteenth century, the evangelist D.L. Moody and his wife Emma. It was their niece, Louise, who said of them: *Aunt Emma and Uncle Dwight were so perfectly* **one***, that no one could possibly tell which was* **the** *one!* [9]

Let us believe that the same courage and confidence that inspired the Christian church of the first century to defy the standards of an entire continent, will resurface in the twenty-first century. It only takes a few, as Paul and his friends were to prove. Say to yourself, *I resolve that it is going to begin with* **me**.

8. Ruth Bell Graham, *Prodigals and those who love them,* Focus on the Family, 1991, p. 102.
9. John Pollock, *Moody without Sankey,* Christian Focus, 1995, p.261.

12

'Is that it?'

(Rock musician Bob Geldof, 13 July 1985)

In a rain-drenched and packed Wembley Stadium, the lightning had already hit one of the famous twin towers as Billy Graham ended a month of meetings in London. His subject had been the life resolve of the apostle Paul, *God forbid that I should glory, save in the Cross of our Lord Jesus Christ.* At the close, several thousand men and women crossed the pitch in response to the call of Christ, many of them holding their shoes in their hands as they splashed their way towards the platform. One of the evangelist's closing points had been taken from the bestselling book of the Irish rock singer Bob Geldof. As Billy delivered the punchline, I recollected that my colleagues Pam Glover and Miranda Lewis had arranged to send the book to Dr Graham from our church office, in response to a request from his hotel. The words boomed around Wembley with telling effect:

Only a few years ago, in this same great stadium, 'Live Aid' – the biggest concert of all time – was staged by Bob Geldof and music makers from all over the world. When it was over, some young fans, at the foot of the platform, shouted up to the organisers: *'Is that it?'* And Bob Geldof wrote, as the final sentence in his book: *'It's something I keep asking myself.'* The words became the title of his book – *'Is that it?'*

Many of you, as you look at the emptiness of your own lives, are asking the same question: *Is that it? Is that all there is to life upon this world?* I'm here to bring you the thrilling announcement that there's more!

Even the cleverest people, from early days of our civilisation, have been asking the same question about the purpose of our lives here: *Is that it?* Aristotle's last prayer has come down to us from the fourth century BC:

I entered the world corruptly,
I have lived in it anxiously,
I quit it in perturbation.

In our modern era, after the great triumph of sailing around the world in his boat *Gipsy Moth IV*, Sir Francis Chichester described his feelings when the celebrations were all over: 'I saw myself as a trickle of water draining away into a sandy beach, leading to a dead-end. Life itself seemed futile.'[1]

Is that it? Of all people on earth, it ought to be the believer who displays a confidence about the meaning of life, the direction of our human story – and the way in which it will all end! If we look at the people who shaped the collective thinking of our civilisation, we discover that – whatever the political or cultural confusions that swirled around them – they all had a God-centred world-view, and their thought processes were based on the Bible. Irenaeus, Augustine, Erasmus, Luther and Tolstoy are all prime examples. If Bible concepts and idioms were to be outlawed from our society tomorrow, all the great music and literature that have formed our culture would become meaningless overnight. The works of William Shakespeare would be indecipherable.

It is ingrained deeply in our thought forms. And basic Christian belief embraces a view of the universal and permanent kingdom of God as something that straddles every empire that has come and gone. It finds a remarkable focus in the inspired leadership of a Jew who lived twenty-six centuries ago – the prophet Daniel. Starting as a young, teenage captive in the alien Babylonian court of Nebuchadnezzar, Daniel was to rise to a stardom and an influence that still shines like a comet in our present era, as the second

1. Sir Francis Chichester, *Gipsy Moth Circles the World,* Hodder & Stoughton, 1967, p. 222.

millennium gives way to the third. *Where is our story going? When is it going to end? How can people manage when chaos seems to rule, and when barbarians are occupying the seats of power?* Daniel had seen it all, as the fortunes of his people, the Jews, seemed to trickle away into the sandy wastes of a terrible seventy-year captivity in Babylon. **'Is that it?'** was the agonised cry of the ancient people of God.

The book of Daniel, from the very first chapter – when the Famous Four challenged the lifestyle of Nebuchadnezzar's heathen court – has a consistent theme: *How should God's people behave in an alien land?* It is a question we have always had to face throughout spiritual history, for all believers are 'strangers and pilgrims' in a world that has turned its back upon the rule of God. We find ourselves echoing the question of the captives in Psalm 137 – 'How can we sing the Lord's song in a foreign land?'

Like Daniel we are called, as citizens of heaven, to a life of **integrity**, whatever our surroundings. Daniel's friends face the fiery furnace; he himself is thrown into a den of lions – but through it all there is no inconsistency between Daniel's private and public behaviour. He shows the whole world how it's done! Furthermore, in the twelve riveting chapters that make up Daniel's prophecy, there is an insistent call to **stability**, as we watch the way in which a leader for God can outlive kingdom after tumbling kingdom. Dictator follows dictator, crisis follows crisis; and yet *'Daniel remained'* (Dan. 1:21).

There is also the theme of **humility** that weaves its way through the prophecy, as the reader is confronted by the key truth that 'the Most High rules in the kingdoms of men'. That was the message stamped upon chapter 2 and the dream of the great metal statue, representing the toppling kingdoms of this world. It was the great testimony that came out of the madness of King Nebuchadnezzar in chapter 4. It was the stark reality behind the terrifying 'writing on the wall' that heralded the collapse of Belshazzar's kingdom in a single night. It was the basis of Daniel's own vision of the evil beasts and the shining figure of the Son of Man in chapter 7. It was the reassuring background to chapter 8, with its vision of the apparently unstoppable he-goat of the Greek rise to power. It is God's hammer blow upon *the Abomination that causes Desolation* – the sinister personage who features so prominently in these chapters as a prefigure of the final Antichrist. All will be brought down, as the small stone of chapter 2 – uncut by human hand – smashes into the kingdoms of this world and reduces them to fragments, itself growing to the size of a mountain that fills the whole earth. It is a vision of the kingdom of God that will never be destroyed!

It is at the close of the prophecy, in chapter 12, that we can share a little of Daniel's telescopic view, as an angelic messenger brings 'the time of the end' into focus:

At that time Michael, the great prince who protects your people, will arise. There will be a time of distress such as has not happened from the beginning of nations until then. But at that time your people – everyone whose name is found written in the book – will be delivered. Multitudes who sleep in the dust of the earth will awake: some to everlasting life, others to shame and everlasting contempt. Those who are wise will shine like the brightness of the heavens, and those who lead many to righteousness, like the stars for ever and ever. But you, Daniel, close up and seal the words of the scroll until the time of the end...(Dan. 12:1-4).

In this passage and the rest of chapter 12, some contrasts are given, to sharpen the focus of all God's people as we wait for 'the end'. They are there to energise us in the period of endurance and waiting that confronts every generation of believers.

The tribulation and the deliverance

'Michael' (v.1), that angelic figure – associated in Revelation 12 with the victory of Christ over all evil – is presented here as the great contestant on behalf of God's people, during the time of their greatest trial. It is thought by many Bible students that the New Testament letter to the Hebrews, in its eleventh chapter, is referring back to the terrible time of Greek ascendancy in the second century BC – when the notorious Seleucid leader, Antiochus Epiphanes, made war upon the Jews in his kingdom: *They were stoned; they were sawn in two; they were put to death by the sword...'* (Heb. 11:37).

But these trials were the curtain-raiser for further and even more terrible persecutions that were to be the story of the church's life until the end of time. There is a certain running-together, a telescoping of events in Daniel's prophecy. Jesus did the same in his warning of the destruction of Jerusalem that lay ahead in AD70. He described it in terms of 'great distress, unequalled from the beginning of the world until now and never to be equalled again'. But he linked the event with the trials that will be the prelude to the end of the world; trials so great that – as he put it – 'If those days had not been cut short, no-one would survive, but for the sake of the elect those days will be shortened' (Matt. 24:21, 22).

Antiochus-like antichrist figures will keep surfacing throughout history, usurping the place of God and oppressing his people. They will culminate in what the apostle Paul describes as the 'Man of Lawlessness', who will finally be overthrown at Christ's return and judgment (2 Thess. 2:1-12). It is perhaps understandable that at certain times in history, people are tempted to try and identify the Antichrist. But we are better advised to turn full attention upon *Christ*. He is our proper focal point.

We will never be without trials. At the same time Daniel emphasises the eternal security of those whose names are found written in 'the book'. As we saw in an earlier chapter, the 'two witnesses' will triumph. Followers of Christ have never ceased to be amazed at the continuance of the church, despite every indication that its light was about to be extinguished. *The tribulation and the deliverance* – the two themes run together throughout the Bible, and those with an eye for history will see the pattern amply confirmed again and again.

The wise and the wicked

Verse 2 of Daniel 12 refers to the 'multitudes' who comprise the human race. The prophet describes them as divided into two classes. There are *only* two classes – you are either in one or the other!

First, **the wise**. We learn in verse 3 that they shine like the stars of heaven. Who are they? Why they are those who know and fear God – for it is the fear of the Lord that is the beginning of wisdom. They are people like Lorna Bowden of my childhood missionary background. Such people are remembered, long after the departure of others. When I went to preach at our old home church of Weithaga in Kenya during the 1990s, Lorna Bowden was still remembered from decades earlier. Several generations of Christian workers had lived in her house since the time when I knew her as a boy. But to this day the little stone bungalow with the corrugated iron roof is known by one and all as *Miss Bowden's house*. If such 'stars' as Auntie Lorna endure in the memory of God's people, we can be sure that she – who 'led many to righteousness' – will shine in the firmament of God for ever and ever.

Against the wise are **the wicked**. They occur later in our Scripture passage:

> Many will be purified, made spotless and refined, but the wicked will continue to be wicked. None of the wicked will understand, but those who are wise will understand (Dan. 12:10).

We should not imagine that the wicked cannot change sides in this life; Nebuchadnezzar was one who did! (Dan. 4:37). At the same time it must be recognised that the coming judgment of God serves to underline the choices that people were making throughout a lifetime. 'Let him who does wrong continue to do wrong; let him who is vile continue to be vile' (Rev. 22:11). It will become apparent, on the day of judgment, who were allotted a place with the wise and who a place with the wicked.

Glorification and judgment

Such a contrast – again, it's one or the other! Bible students should be grateful for verse 2; it provides one of the clearest references in the Old Testament to the glory of everlasting life and the resurrection of God's people. We are going, by God's grace, to rise again. It's there in the Old Testament, and Jesus is the historical guarantee that it is going to happen! Without the Bible revelation before us, we would be completely in the dark about the next life. As intellectual a sage as Xenophanes had said in the sixth century BC, *Guesswork is over all.*

But again at this point there is a separation. The wise will rise to the glorified state of everlasting life; the wicked to everlasting contempt and judgment. You can be best friends, or exact contemporaries – but still be heading towards different destinies. The nineteenth-century preacher, D.L. Moody of Chicago, has featured in an earlier chapter. His contemporary in America was a professed agnostic by the name of Robert Ingersoll. Independently of each other, the two men toured America ceaselessly, one preaching Christ, the other promoting unbelief. Both died in the same year, 1899. When Moody died, on 21 December, memorial and thanksgiving services were held, and the best of the Sankey hymns reverberated through the land. Ingersoll died on 21 July, and – while it is not for us to be his judge – we can only note that by contrast his earlier memorial had included the stark notice, *There will be no singing.* Glorification and judgment: the Bible warns us to look ahead, and to prepare.

The revealed and the hidden

In the last part of Daniel's twelfth chapter, the seer is aware of the presence of a 'man clothed in linen', seemingly identical to the shining figure of chapter 10. If so, then he is the pre-incarnate second Person of the Trinity. Jesus is accompanied by two angelic beings:

> One of them said to the man clothed in linen, who was above the waters of the river, 'How long will it be before these astonishing things are fulfilled?'... So I asked, 'My lord, what will the outcome of all this be?' (Dan. 12:6, 8).

Two questions are being posed to the Man in shining linen. They amount to:

How long must we wait?
How will it all end?

We might have put it differently. 'Is anything going to change? Is there anything more? *Is that it?*'

The answers to both questions help us in our Christian living today. To the first *How long?* comes the answer, 'It will be for a time, times and half a time. When the power of the holy people has been finally broken, all these things will be completed' (Dan. 12:7). The three and a half 'years', symbolic of both the oppression and powerful witness of Elijah's time (1 Kings 18:1; cf. James 5:17) is applied in the book of Revelation to the whole of our Christian era. It is an era in which we may *expect* to see the kingdom of God advancing – despite inevitable opposition, and even the ultimate and apparent 'breaking' of the church and its power. It is at 'the time of the end', when things are looking at their worst, that all God's purposes are 'completed', and the Son of Man comes to claim his kingdom in universal power (Dan. 7:13, 14).

And to the question of the final outcome, the message is firm and practical: 'Go your way, Daniel, because the words are closed up and sealed until the time of the end' (Dan. 12:9). It amounts to an assurance that the prophet is to receive all that God has revealed, and is to remain humble and patient over what remains sealed (vv.4,9).

Patience is the name of the game! The divine message to Daniel is, 'Get on with your life and task. You know enough to realise that there is more to what you can see taking place in the present distress'. **'As for you, go your way till the end'** (Dan. 12:13).

Jesus was to say something similar to the apostle Peter, during the post-Resurrection breakfast on the beach. Peter had been commissioned for service, but then asked questions about his colleague John. 'What is that to you?' replied Jesus, *'You must follow me'* (John 21:22).

Is that it? We know enough to recognise that there is more to what is going on than petrol prices, mortgage loans, job losses – and the lurching of nations from crisis to crisis. As the old millenium was giving way to the new, there was a rise in tension and excitement. There were crazy books and the irrational antics of religious extremists, infected by psychic epidemics that sweep our world. The crazes continue, but a sense of let-down began to set in. Had anything really changed? *Was that it?*

The call is to stand with the Son of Man, who knows the end from the beginning, to identify with God's people in the church and to see this present age through to its completion.

In the Greek epic, *The Iliad,* written by Homer over seven hundred years before Christ, the war against Troy is vividly described. It's the story of Agamemnon, leader of the combined Greek forces. In it we are given the account of the placing of a sentinel – to keep watch, year after year, for the beacon blaze signalling that Troy, at last, had been taken. Time rolls by.... ten years in all; until one memorable day the strategy of the famous Wooden Horse brings victory. At long last the announcement flares up and is relayed from hill to hill, and reflected in the waves of the Aegean Sea. Then, and only then, as the news arrives, *Troy has fallen,* is the sentinel informed, **'Your duty is done. The long wait is over; you are relieved.'**

Carey Francis was perhaps the greatest educationist that Kenya ever had. I knew him only as Uncle Carey. He was the headmaster of Nairobi's famed Alliance High School. His impact upon the country's leadership was enormous. When he died, hundreds of his former pupils, including members of the Kenya Cabinet, turned out to carry and escort his coffin to the grave, filling it in with their own hands. He once said, 'When I go, I want God to find me with my letters answered, my work up to date, *and me hard at it.*'

As for you, go your way till the end.
You will rest, and then at the end of the days
you will rise to receive your allotted inheritance

13

'To those who say that
our city will never
be the same I say, "You
are right. It will
be better"'

(Mayor Rudolph Giuliani of
New York,
23 September 2001)

'Look, Liz, helicopters everywhere'. We were emerging from our rented villa into the sunshine of Wednesday, 12 September 2001. My wife and I were on Naxos, one of innumerable little Greek islands scattered throughout the Aegean Sea. You go there for a quiet holiday in the sun, travelling from Athens by hovercraft. Nothing at all happens on Naxos.

The whirling helicopters from the mainland said it all that morning. Security had suddenly become an issue even on a remote Aegean island. Something of world-reverberating proportions had taken place the day before, thousands of miles away in New York. But we already knew this, even on the very day of 'Nine Eleven' – as our American friends came to call the terrorist attack on the World Trade Centre. Within a few hours of the atrocity, on a decrepit TV set in the corner of a waterfront *taberna* we were seeing the CNN News, with flickering Greek captions, as we paid for our meal. If even Naxos knows this, I thought to myself, then the whole world must know it.

It was brought home to me a day or two later at Athens' airport – when even my inoffensive nail scissors were confiscated before we were allowed to board the plane for London.

'Nothing sharp must be allowed on the flight,' the Greek official gravely explained.

I was itching to get back to the family and to All Souls Church. At the church my colleague Paul Williams had already made alterations to the programme; he had opened up the church on the evening of the fateful Tuesday for a special service of prayers. During our flight, thoughts kept returning to the hideous images of violence – and to the mindset of its perpetrators. How can someone be 'filled with joy' and 'praise Allah' at the sight of bodies falling out of a skyscraper?

Unbidden, a quotation from Blaise Pascal floats into my mind: *Men never do evil so completely and cheerfully as when they do it from religious conviction.*

We consume a Greek salad on the Olympic Air flight. Now it's Solzhenitsyn who infiltrates my thinking. He had spoken in London on receiving the Templeton Award years ago. Snatches from his memorable speech come back to me:

> It has already come to pass that the demon of evil, like a whirlwind, triumphantly circles all five continents of the earth... It is during such trials that the highest gifts of the human spirit are manifested. If we perish and lose the world, the fault will be ours alone.

Already some of those gifts of the human spirit were manifesting themselves in the face of Nine/Eleven. In another Greek *taberna* we had already seen and heard an inspired Billy Graham, invited by President Bush to participate in the memorial service, transmitted live from Washington to the whole world. He had spoken compellingly of the confidence that stems from the Cross and Resurrection of Christ. Stories of heroism were now beginning to hit the public: the 343 firefighters who perished under the rubble in Lower Manhattan... Todd Beamer on Flight 93, who asked the telephone operator to pray with him before rushing the attackers, and his last recorded words – 'Are you ready, guys? Let's roll'.

And there was Rudy's moment. Trudging through the smoking ruins – FDNY cap firmly on his head in identification with the decimated fire department – calming and inspiring his fellow New Yorkers, speaking before the cameras with precision and purpose, Mayor Giuliani was voted Man of the Year in *Time* magazine. No one grudged the honorary Knighthood that the Queen was later to confer upon him.

'God bless you!' he would encourage the tireless workers at Ground Zero. It was on 23 September, that he came out with the statement that titles this chapter: **'To those who say that our city will never be the same I say, "You are right. It will be better."'**

Notwithstanding the unknown future outcome of the protracted conflict with world terrorism, Mayor Giuliani's leadership voiced the 'Can Do' outlook of America. Shallow, and even brash, some may call it – but such optimism contrasts boldly with the tired cynicism that so often drip-feeds its way into public life on the other side of the Atlantic.

The American spirit arrived on the wings of the Puritan exodus from the dank oppression of seventeenth-century Europe. The Pilgrim Fathers were pursuing their destiny as the Chosen People – to breach frontiers, to found a paradise of God in a new land. **'We shall be as a city upon a hill'**, exulted Governor John Winthrop of Massachusetts Bay Colony in 1630. He was quoting from the Sermon on the Mount, and his sentiment was not dissimilar from Rudy Giuliani's.

It is not all empty bravado, though America is no paradise. The Bible – on which the world-view of the Puritans was based – speaks of a Homeland that ever beckons the chosen faithful. It did so, back in the days of Isaiah the prophet, over seven hundred years before the birth of Jesus. The Jewish people had been oppressed first by the Assyrians, then by the Babylonians. Only with the ascendancy of the Medo-Persians were the Jews to be freed from their captivity, and given a mandate to begin the great trek home:

> They that wait upon the Lord will renew their strength; they shall mount up with wings as eagles; they shall run and not be weary; and they shall walk and not faint. (Isaiah 40:31 KJV)

Today's 'whirlwind of evil' found a focus that 11 September, when organised terrorism brazenly threatened the destiny and peace of an entire civilisation. Money markets were closed down, air flights grounded and weapons systems placed on high alert.

Question: Does civilisation in the West possess within itself a cohesive philosophy and world-view, credible enough and powerful enough both to withstand the pressures of current world evil, and to attract the rest of humanity with its appeal?

The answer, for a long time, has quite clearly been 'No'. The West may have the affluence and the weaponry, but the world has never been effectively changed by anything other than ideas. Old style Socialism, closely allied to Communism, was bound to fail the twentieth century, with its legacy of collapsed economies, religious persecution and crushed freedoms. But Capitalism, too, was destined to disappoint its advocates, despite its competitive edge and materialist attractions. It has spoken with the language of profit, choice and ownership, but has nevertheless been devoid of power to stem the tide of violence and drug abuse, divorce, urban poverty, and moral chaos.

There then entered Bill Clinton and Tony Blair. Their quest for what has been called a Third Way aimed at a modernised social democracy – pragmatic and flexible – aiming for a reformed welfare state and greater inclusiveness of life. Granted that their programme – unlike the others – possessed only a limited intellectual rationale – it has nevertheless held a certain appeal for a number of European political leaders.

But it will fail for the very same reasons that Marxism and Capitalism faltered. *All three programmes began with the axiomatic assumption that God does not exist.* The church is permitted to operate, of course – but only in a sidelined existence as one of a number of religious groups which must be effectively *contained.*

Lord Griffiths of Fforestfach made the point, during a speech in New York, that 'A Third Way without religious renewal will founder on the same rocks of secularism that have wrecked both socialism and capitalism' *(To the Christian Ministries to the UN Community, 16 March 1999).*

The lesson is not going to be learnt by the proponents of this Third Way – not while they continue in oblivion of the historical processes that gave Europe and America their cultural and spiritual foundation. They seem to be completely ignorant of Augustine's *City of God* – a mighty work which moulded Europe over an entire millennium. It is as though Jerome, Augustine's contemporary, had never produced the Vulgate – a common-language version of the Bible that, similarly, was to span the continent for a thousand years. Art and education, exploration and invention, politics and basic citizenship all owed their development to these powerful forces.

Many modern leaders appear to be unaware of the spiritual and cultural effects of the Reformation – even though the erected memorials to its martyrs still stand today. And the Pilgrim Fathers? Why, they would be an embarrassment to any Third Way advocate who knew of the Christian convictions underlying that historic voyage to the New World. And what of the powerful Clapham group reformers under John Venn and William Wilberforce? Or Moody and Sankey – whose *Sacred Songs and Solos* sold a breathtaking eighty million copies? These pivotal shapers of ethics and values across great tracts of the world might never have existed. Europe confidently expects to build a cohesive unity among its member countries, while busying itself with throwing out the spiritual influences that gave it a common culture in the first place.

All this means that – if Solzhenitsyn's fear of 'losing' the world is to be relieved – a rejuvenated church will have to do it, *and the church is likely to be out there on its own*. This, in itself, is no bad thing.

It is not that others are completely powerless in the stand against world wide evil. It is simply that we need a bigger framework of thinking than could ever be provided from the micro-world of Mayor Giuliani's New York. Given that Americans will display optimistic vigour against determined opponents – as contrasted with European hesitation – history has shown that unprincipled evil cannot really be combated by patriotic fervour alone, nor even by a militaristic show down. In ultimate terms America, as a nation, can be defiant, but only relatively defiant.

The world-view created by the Scriptures would come down on the side of Lord Griffiths' analysis. '*Not by might, nor by power, but my my Spirit*', was the divine message given to the Jewish people, when flirting with militarism as the talisman of success (Zechariah 4:6). The controlled use of force – as distinguished from violence – can be a useful policeman, but it has no power whatever to influence the permanent thinking – and therefore lifestyle – of vast numbers of people.

How, then, to stand against evil, when we see it on a surge everywhere around us?

Isaiah was another Old Testament prophet who knew the answer some twenty-seven centuries ago. *And his was the big view.* Like other giants of civilisation, he was able to step back and see the whole picture. And, like them, he knew how evil can be outfaced, in his God-given analysis:

When the enemy shall come in like a flood, the Spirit of the Lord shall lift up a standard against him (Isaiah 59:19 KJV) .

Yes, we should favour the King James Version for this text of Scripture – and not simply because these words have encouraged generations of believers, caught in the firestorms ignited by the antichrists of history; but because the King James version evidently has the correct translation. Modern versions place the emphasis of Isaiah 59:19 on *the Lord* coming in like a pent-up flood, driven by the divine Spirit. But the modern Bible commentator, Alec Motyer, reinstates the King James translation at this point. The word for 'enemy' is the same Hebrew word as in the previous verse – where the sentence is very clearly referring to the evil adversaries of God.

Confronted by a flood of evil, *the Spirit of the Lord shall lift up a standard against him.* The use of the personal pronoun is striking. We are dealing with a person. *Him.* From beginning to end, the teaching of the Bible is that the intrusion of evil into our affairs is far more profound than an assortment of unfortunate circumstances, which – by a process of evolving ethics or altered structures – the human race can learn to conquer.

Professor C.E.M. Joad gained an enormous following in the first half of the twentieth century, through his broadcasts on British radio. For most of his life at London's Birkbeck College, he had identified with the theorists who held that evil can be dealt with as a problem *only* of outward circumstance. The 'growing pains' of the human race could, surely, be overcome, given time. Joad wrote, in all, forty-seven books.

But he back tracked the year before he died. In his last book, *Recovery of Belief,* he admitted that this entire built-up theory 'has been rendered utterly unplausible by the events of the last forty years'. He was referring to the experience of two world wars:

'To me, at any rate, the view of evil implied by Marxism, expressed by [George Bernard] Shaw and maintained by modern psychotherapy, a view which regards evil as a by-product of circumstances, which circumstances can therefore alter and even eliminate, has come to seem intolerably shallow.'

It had taken the professor a lifetime and forty-seven books finally to arrive at this conclusion that ties in with the biblical testimony.

As the billowing smoke over lower Manhattan turned day to night in Church Street, the thought became inescapable: If we take out the influence of Christ, we have not changed at all since day one of the Fall! Ground Zero in New York... the scandal of Enron.... the Bulger murder in Britain... the St James' Church massacre in Cape Town....the genocide of Sudan... of Bosnia... of Rwanda... the torture chambers of Pinochet... the killing fields of Cambodia – *didn't we leave all that behind in Auschwitz?*

No, we didn't – neither in Lockerbie, Eniskillin or the Waco siege in Texas. Time after time the cry has gone up, 'It must never happen again!'...'The war to end all wars!' Solzhenitsyn – again – touched a nerve when he declared in London, 'Today's world has reached a stage which, if it had been described to preceding centuries, would have called forth the cry, "This is the Apocalypse!"'

In point of fact, similar observations have been made all along the high roads of history. As far back as the oppressive reign of King Stephen in twelfth-century England, the common conclusion reached was that 'God and his angels slept'.

Back then to Isaiah. Confronted as he and his people were by the menacing might of Assyria, this discerning prophet was able to stand back from the darkening scene and see it against the wider picture of God and his over-arching rule in all our human affairs. To see the end from the beginning! If I can do that in the modern world, then – like those ancient seers – I can learn to create a raft with which to negotiate a way through the rocks and the currents of apparently uncontrollable forces.

And my raft is composed of four mighty planks. In his book *New Issues Facing Christians Today* (IVP, 1999), John Stott draws attention to the four great epochs – or events – of Bible history. They are Creation, the Fall, Redemption and the Consummation (or final Triumph). With these as the planks that make up my raft, I can not only survive the floodtides of evil – using the four epochs as a basic framework with which to understand the whole of life – I can do more! With such a world-view, Christ is seen as the origin, substance and goal of all history. This knowledge inspires me to take an active part in a worldwide fellowship of the Spirit, as the standard is lifted up in the fight against evil. This is where the church comes in.

The implication of Isaiah 59:19 is that God does it all. The prophet powerfully portrays him as the great protagonist and fighter. Yet he chooses to involve us; he will look for that person who, in any given situation, will still be standing in the breach, when the dam holding back evil seems to give way, and great swirling waters are released.

When error and evil are rampaging unchecked, the temptation is, mentally and spiritually, to give up. The enemy is so strong, *and he is a person.*

However, we should be encouraged by the undergirding of the four planks. Evil was not there from eternity – as God and goodness are. If evil was eternally co-existent with goodness, then the French writer Baudelaire might have been right in his words, 'If there is a god, he is the devil' (*Les Fleurs du Mal*).

But chapters 1-3 of Genesis cut that blasphemous argument off. Evil originates neither in eternity, nor in goodness. Augustine reinforced the argument:

> 'The evil angels, though created good, became evil
> by their voluntary defection from the good, so that
> the cause of evil is not the good, but defection from
> the good' *(The City of God,* Book 12, chapter 9*)*

And the Fall has been followed by God's Redemption in the sacrificial death of Jesus Christ and in the consequent pledge of the final triumph of goodness over evil. Evil, which came as an intrusion into the world, will have a decisive end! The Bible smashes to pieces the error of 'dualism' – the belief in two equal and eternal systems, good and evil, existing permanently side by side. Goodness – which is for ever – will have the final word. This should inspire prayer and optimistic hope, on the part of relief agencies and missions everywhere, no matter what the aggravation.

The four planks teach me that when the enemy comes in like a flood, we who have aligned ourselves with Christ are working and witnessing, not towards victory, but *from* victory, already achieved at the Cross. The final outcome is assured, once we have read the last page in the Bible. For this reason, the apparently feeble church has outlasted every institution that has threatened it. It is with confidence, then, that we gather under 'the standard' that the Spirit of the Lord shall lift up.

What is this standard? Isaiah himself gives us the answer as he writes of the distant future:

> 'In that day, the Root of Jesse will stand as a banner for the peoples; the nations will rally to him, and his place of rest will be glorious. He will raise a banner for the nations, and gather the exiles of Israel; he will assemble the scattered people of Judah from the four corners of the earth'   (Isaiah 11:10–12)

Him. It's personal. 'The Root of Jesse' is a reference to the coming Christ. Yes, although he was a descendant of Jesse – King David's father – yet he is also ancestor. He is the 'root' as well as the 'offspring' (Revelation 22:16) – he is the very ancestor of the ancestors! It is the eternal figure of Christ, then, who personifies the powerful 'standard' against the flooding in of evil.

A standard is a symbol of war. Did the Christian expect anything other than conflict, on responding to the call for discipleship? Even so, the battle against the power of evil was won, through the death of the Cross; the victory only remains to be *consummated.* For this reason the Devil is 'filled with fury, because he knows that his time is short'

(Revelation 12:12). Hence, the intensity of the current struggle. No Christian believer is exempt from it.

A standard is a symbol of unity. Recruits enlist around a standard. Combatants, aware of their own weakness, will flock to a common banner that they love and recognise. Never mind whether we are Baptists, Episcopalians or Presbyterians! I was intensely aware of this unity at Billy Graham's great *Amsterdam 2000* congress for preaching evangelists from around the world. There we were, over eleven thousand of us – drawn from no less than 211 nations. *It was the most internationally-representative gathering, secular or religious, in the whole of history*. We were a living illustration of Christ's words in John 12:22, 'But I, when I am lifted up from the earth, will draw all men to myself'. A holy unity descended upon us from day one of that powerful assembly, poised – as Dr Graham put it – 'to light again a fire of love and truth that would never go out'.

A standard is a symbol of conquest. Originally the Cross of Jesus resembled an emblem of defeat and death. But no longer. The demonic powers of all the ages converged upon that limp figure upon the Cross, yet there 'he made a public spectacle of them, triumphing over them by the cross' (Colossians 2:15).

A standard is a symbol of direction. 'Forward March!' is the message. Christ is the Rider on the white horse of Revelation 19:11–16, leading the armies of heaven arrayed in fine linen. The message of the Revelation shines like a comet across the centuries to all who have suffered under the onslaught of evil. *No one can stop Jesus.*

It's Christ who is the key. Catastrophe is never going to

have the last say. Tyranny rarely lasts beyond its own regime. The entire apparatus of evil will be dismantled at the end, leaving the church – through Christ and Christ alone – standing over its smoking grave.

RICHARD BEWES

INCLUDES GUIDE FOR GROUP STUDY

THE
STONE
THAT BECAME A
MOUNTAIN

Getting it RIGHT about the Kingdom of God

'One of the most important books I have read' David Bushet

The Stone that became a Mountain
Getting it RIGHT About the Kingdom
Richard Bewes

'In today's changing world, where nations rise and fall, leaders come and go, thrones are occupied and emptied, treaties are made and broken, and life itself seems so fragile, The Stone that became a Mountain is the telescope that brings into focus the unchanging, transcending kingdom of God. Well done, Richard Bewes!'
Anne Graham Lotz of Angel Ministries

'The Stone that became a Mountain' is truly inspired. It has become for me one of the most important and helpful books I have read in recent years.' **David Suchet, Actor**

'The Kingdom of God is a non negotiable in Christian understanding. Have you grasped it? Nothing else so clearly shapes Christian thinking. This is **the** book - laced with vivid illustration - to explain this essential Christian truth.' **Rico Tice,**

Beginning with the prophet Daniel's glowing imagery of the stone that grew into a mountain, Richard Bewes has come up with a colourful - and vital - presentation of the biggest thing there is; the kingdom that outlives and outlasts everything else in sight.

'Get the teaching *wrong*,' says Richard, 'and you land yourself in a traffic-jam of errors which will affect just about everything you ever do or touch. But get it *right*, and you'll be able to hold your own - and win - in the face of the false ideologies and alien teachings that are flooding our world in the twenty-first century.'

ISBN 1 85792 714 1   176 pages
Published 2001

'Makes Revelation's central lines of thought leap to life and relevance.'
Don Carson

The Lamb Wins!
A guided tour through
The Book of Revelation

RICHARD BEWES
NEW EDITION

The Lamb Wins
A Guided Tour through
the book of Revelation
Richard Bewes

What is the average person to make of the book of Revelation? Richard Bewes steers his readers through the minefields of bizarre interpretations and picks out the great themes that are the message of Christ to every generation of believers. Whilst suitable for newcomers to the Christian faith, pastors have also used it to give them confidence to preach through Revelation.

'The Lamb Wins' can also be used as 6 group studies, complete with study questions

ISBN 1 85792 597 1   160 pages trade
Published 2000

RICHARD BEWES

TALKING ABOUT PRAYER
'God bless you as you read this book.'
Billy Graham

Talking about Prayer
Richard Bewes

"I hope that this readable little book will find its way into the hands of Christian people on every continent, for it will have an immediate appeal to thousands who are rediscovering the life of prayer, both individually and through prayer groups.

"Learn the secret of prayer! Through Christ we can find in God a heavenly Father, who hears and answers prayer. It is true to say that anyone who has ever advanced as a Christian and whose life counted for the kingdom of God has been a person of prayer.

"It is my firm belief that Talking about Prayer could significantly strengthen the invisible network of praying people that God has brought into being around our world. God bless you as you read this book."

Billy Graham

'I would never have chosen to write a book on the prayer life. What a subject – and how hypocritical one feels in making the attempt! This cannot be an exhaustive treatise; the very idea that anyone could cover the whole field of prayer in a kind of technical manual is ridiculous. But there might be some simple guidelines in these pages that can be put to use in your churches and fellowship groups. I have deliberately tried to let each chapter stand on its own, so that the reader can feel easy about dipping into the pages at random.'

Richard Bewes

ISBN 1 85792 6137   160 pages mass market
Published 2000

SPEAKING
IN PUBLIC
EFFECTIVELY

HOW TO PREPARE ▪ HOW TO PRESENT ▪ HOW TO PROGRESS

RICHARD BEWES

Speaking in Public Effectively
How to Prepare, How to Present, How to Progress
Richard Bewes

People fear public speaking more than death!

Surveys show that of all our fears (including death, disease and loneliness) public speaking ranks number one. If standing in front of a room full of people, intent on every word you say, strikes fear into the core of your being then THIS is the book for you.

Distilled from his lifetime of experience, Richard Bewes, an international conference speaker, offers practical advice that will make public speaking something to enjoy rather than endure. Those who have to teach at Sunday school, speak in a business meeting, motivate the company at a conference, present a project at school, run a youth club or preach from a pulpit will find this book a vital tool.

The next time you have to speak in front of others, first aim for success, then read *'Speaking in Public Effectively'* - it will give you the means to achieve your objective.

> *'The majority of speakers I have heard would benefit enormously by applying the contents of this book'* **David Suchet, Actor**

> *'A Wealth of invaluable principles and practical tips from one of Britain's best known and experienced preachers'* **Rev Joel Edwards, General Director, Evangelical Alliance**

> *'The illustrations and style make the text luminous - as if someone were holding a flashlight on the page. It is a joy to recommend a book that is such a delight to read'* **Ruth Bell Graham (wife of Billy Graham)**

> *"A delight... I only wish someone had given it to me 40 years ago"* **The Church of England Newspaper**

ISBN 1 85792 4002   192 large trade
published in 2002